MW01519451

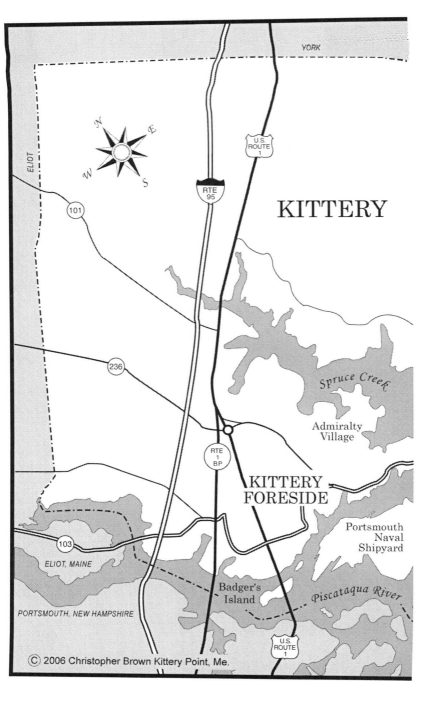

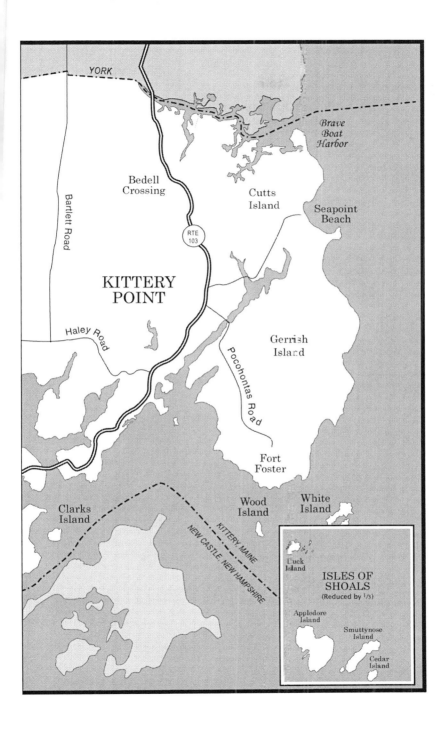

YORK

Brave
Boat
Harbor

Bedell
Crossing

Cutts
Island

Seapoint
Beach

Bartlett Road

RTE
103

KITTERY
POINT

Haley Road

Gerrish
Island

Pocohontas Road

Fort
Foster

Clarks
Island

Wood
Island

White
Island

KITTERY, MAINE
NEW CASTLE, NEW HAMPSHIRE

Duck
Island

ISLES OF
SHOALS
(Reduced by 1/3)

Appledore
Island

Smuttynose
Island

Cedar
Island

KITTERY
GATEWAY TO MAINE

A HISTORY & GUIDE TO
KITTERY & KITTERY POINT

Compiled by the
Friends of the Rice Public Library
Kittery, Maine

back channel press
portsmouth new hampshire
an independent print-on-demand book publisher

BACK CHANNEL PRESS
170 Mechanic Street
Portsmouth, NH 03801
editor@backchannelpress.com
www.backchannelpress.com

Printed in the United States of America
2nd printing, June 2006

Cover and book design by Nancy Grossman

Library of Congress PCN 2005910372

TABLE OF CONTENTS

IMAGE CREDITS

Photographs courtesy of:
>Douglas Armsden: pages v, 26, 29, 32, 62, 81, 95 and 98
>Stephen Delaney: pages 34, 41, 43, 45, 50, 52, 63, 65-6, 68-71, 73, 82, 88 and 107
>Steve Estes: pages 36, 37 and 39
>Nancy Grossman: pages 10 and 76
>Stella Hall: page 31
>Mariners' Museum, Newport News, VA: page 6
>Nan McNally: pages 46, 47, 49, 53-6, 64, 66, 67, 74, 75 and 77
>Portsmouth Naval Shipyard: pages 7, 9, 11, 14-22, 27, 30, 38 and 67
>Neil Troost (Troost Fine Art Photography & Seacoast Impressions; www.troostartphoto. com): page 78
>Windy Burns: pages 72, 79, 83-7 and 89

CAD drawing courtesy of:
>Christopher Brown: page 74

Maps courtesy of:
>Christopher Brown: pages ii-iii and 58-61
>Nancy Grossman: pages 23 and 92-3

Cover aerial photograph also courtesy of the Portsmouth Naval Shipyard

INTRODUCTION & ACKNOWLEDGEMENTS

Why is the "Introduction" the last thing that gets written? It must be human nature. This book has been lovingly put together by seven "Friends of the Rice Public Library" with the intent of creating an extra source of income for the library. We hope we have accomplished this, but it is too soon to tell.

And so the process began. What should it look like? What should be included? What information is important and what information is not? And then we finally got around to the key question: Who is going to read this? Who is going to buy this book? Well, there was much discussion and we finally came to our answer.

This guide book is meant, primarily, to encourage the love of history in our town. Every generation sees history in a different light and this is our view. We hope the old names and old stories come alive again on these pages. After all, Kittery has a great deal of history (1647 to the present day) and a great deal of it is interesting. We hope this book will appeal to all who live in Kittery and Kittery Point.

Our second intention is to enlighten and inform those who are passing through on their way north or south. Have we covered everything? Probably not, but we've made a good beginning. We hope to add to and improve on our guide book in years to come.

This brings us to the acknowledgement and thanks department. First on our long list are Nancy and John Grossman, our publishers in Portsmouth, without whose concrete help and encouragement, this guide book would still be an idea floating around in our heads. And to everyone at the Rice Public Library who e-mailed, faxed, sent books, looked up facts, helped proof-read and were incredibly helpful. And we want to thank the Board of Directors of the Rice Public Library for their dedication to the library and to Barbara Fein who wrote the history of the Rice Library.

We also wish to thank:

* **Christopher Brown** for creating the image of a Bellamy eagle and the most elegant, precise, time-consuming and simply beautiful maps of Kittery and Kittery Point for this book.
* **Barbara Estes** for her help in identifying landmarks on our Tour of Route 103.
* **Steve Estes** for his generous time talking about "Trains, Trolleys and Resort Hotels," and his good suggestions as well as great photographs.
* **Wayne Manson**, curator of the **Kittery Historical and Naval Museum,** for his kind and patient review of many chapters.
* **Ann Beattie**, board member of the **Isles of Shoals Historical and Research Association,** who edited our chapter on the Isles of Shoals and gave her support.
* Photographer **Stephen C. Delaney**, for his creative and artistic images.
* **Douglas Armsden**, for also making his photographic collection available for us to use.
* **Neil Troost**, for the use of one of his superb images.
* The Public Affairs Office of the **Portsmouth Naval Shipyard: Deborah White**, **Gary Hildreth** and especially **Rick Goodfriend** for the wonderful photographs.
* **John B. Hightower**, Director of the **Mariners' Museum** in Newport News, VA, for the use of the Lancaster Eagle photograph and for being a good friend.
* **Gurdon Metz** and **Dean Howells** for a boost that got us started.
* **Marcia Gibbons** for lending a creative hand in the designing of the cover.
* **Rhett Austell** for his hand in proofreading.
* And, last but not least, the families and friends of the undersigned for putting up with us through this past winter.

Carol Austell
Windy Burns
Stella Hall
A. M. McCurdy
Nan McNally
Gurdon Metz
Lezlye Shea

Kittery, ME, 2006

EARLY HISTORY AND SOME OF OUR FOREFATHERS

They came to get land and fish and lumber and minerals, in short to acquire wealth. This is the great motive that in all times has sent forth colonists.

Everett Stackpole, 1903

Twelve miles up the River Dart and across from the town of Dartmouth, England, is a point of land today called Kingsweare. It is known that there was a Kittery Point in Kingsweare and, as many of the early families came from this area (Devonshire), it is speculated that it is here that the name of Kittery originated.

Kittery's coastal location formed a history rich in fishing, trading and shipbuilding. Even the sparse farming and timber businesses were integral parts of the maritime life. Native peoples and possibly the Vikings were in the area before the early 1600's when Europeans began to explore the local shores, islands and the Piscataqua River. **Martin Pring** (1603) and **Samuel de Champlain** (1605) were the earliest known explorers to arrive here followed by **Captain John Smith** (1614). **Smith** sailed to the group of islands off the Kittery shore looking for fishing grounds to support the Virginia settlement. He found an abundant supply of fish and named the group of islands Smith (or Smyth's) Isles which are now known as the **Isles of Shoals**. (See also page 24.) Subsequently, other fishermen came to the Isles from Europe to fish, dry their catch on the rocks and transport this valuable commodity back to the Continent.

The richness of the land and seas attracted the attention of the English and the Crown. By 1639, King Charles I granted a large tract of land to **Sir Ferdinando Gorges** to be developed. That tract comprised what is now the southern part of Maine. Gorges organized the area into parcels of land to be governed by his friends and relatives. Many of these settlers came from the Devon coast of England and replicated the life of the English gentry. **Champernowne** (a Gorges nephew), **Shapleigh** and **Cutts** were the prominent names. Merchants, farmers, fishermen and shipwrights also came to transform this place into an English colony. Kittery was formally organized into a town in 1647 (as the Piscataqua Plantation) which gives it the distinction of being the oldest incorporated town in Maine.

The Massachusetts Puritans, wanting to extend their control beyond the Piscataqua River, approached the earlier inhabitants of the less-developed Kittery settlement and offered them an act known as the "Submission" in 1652, which promised religious tolerance, the right to vote and titles to land in exchange for obedience to Puritan law. Maine became part of Massachusetts for nearly two hundred years until achieving statehood in 1820.

Farming was at first done on a small scale. Corn was sometimes milled on the Piscataqua River for export. Farmers raised cattle and also lived off the local game and fish. As the farms were often located close to the water, shipbuilding became a natural extension of early colonial life.

FRANCIS CHAMPERNOWNE (1614-1687)
As the final leg of an emigration begun at Plymouth seventeen years earlier, **Francis Champernowne** came to America in 1637 at the age of 23, from Dartington in South Devonshire, England. He belonged to an aristocratic family and was Sir Ferdinando Gorge's nephew. He had served as Captain in the Royal Navy. Sir Ferdinando Gorges had been granted vast territories on either side of the Piscataqua River by King Charles I (1639) of England. Champernowne lived on his estate in Greenland, NH, until he inherited 500 acres in Kittery from his father. This large tract of land was known as Champernowne's Island and now is Cutts Island and Gerrish Island. In 1685, he was named a member of Governor Dudley's Council of State, created to govern the lands of New England. He carried on extensive trade out of his warehouse and in wealth and social status ranked higher than any other early settlers. As an elderly man, Champernowne married the widow of Robert Cutts but left no children. He died in 1687 at age 73 and his grave is marked by a cairn on Cutts Island.

THE CUTTS FAMILY
John, Richard, Robert and their sister **Anne Cutt** (or Cutts;

you will find this family referred to both ways) were the forebears of an enterprising family who immigrated to these shores from Wales in the early 1600's, probably to earn their fortune and not because of persecution (see page 24). John was one of the first selectmen mentioned in Portsmouth, NH, records. Richard lived in New Castle where he sold fish from the Isles of Shoals. In 1660, he built and commanded the first fort on the site of what is now Fort Constitution. Robert lived in Barbados for awhile and probably did business with his brothers in New England, receiving fish and lumber in exchange for West India goods. He came to Portsmouth and then moved to Kittery where he established a shipyard and built many ships. He died in 1674. He and his second wife Mary Hoel had six children and after 1674, when a widow, she married Francis Champernowne. Cutts Island was named for this family.

DR. RENALD FERNALD (1595 - 1656)

Dr. Renald Fernald, born around 1595 in Bristol, England, arrived in America in 1630 on the ship **HMS WARWICK** and settled in Kittery. He was the surgeon for a company of colonists sent by Mason & Gorges from England. He became town clerk in 1640 and recorder of deeds in 1654, until his death in 1656. He and his wife Joanna had seven children. It is said that their descendents number fifty thousand.

WILLIAM BADGER (1752 - 1830)

One of six sons in this sixth generation of Badgers in the New World, **William Badger** started as a shipwright during the Revolutionary War. After the war he built his own shipyard on what is now Badger's Island. The war created a great need for ships, and our new Continental Navy commissioned the **USS RANGER** for John Paul Jones and the **USS AMERICA,** which was given to France. His work was continued by his nephew, **Captain Samuel Augustus Badger** (1794-1857), who built over fifty ships in the same shipyard.

DANIEL GOODWIN (?-1712)

As one of the early settlers of Kittery, **Daniel Goodwin** signed the Submission of 1652, joining Kittery to the Massachusetts Bay Colony for defense but maintaining relative independence for religious practice. From 1694 to 1697, Goodwin, as a selectman of Kittery, petitioned the Massachusetts Bay Colony to protect the settlers from Indian attacks, along with a plea to reduce taxes. Many settlers and their children were killed or kidnapped by Indians throughout the late 1600s.

THE DENNETT FAMILY

In 1698, **John Dennett** bought his land in Kittery and built a garrison homestead to protect his family and his near neighbors from Indian attacks during the French and Indian War (1754-1763). A garrison house was one where the second floor overhung the first and was fortified against attack. By the fourth generation, the Hon. **Mark Dennett** (1786-1883) was one of the most influential men in the history of Kittery. He taught grammar school here until he was sixty. He was very interested in local history and left many papers that our famous Everett Stackpole (*Old Kittery and Her Families*) found very helpful. He held many local and state offices and Stackpole says of him, "He was a statesman and a scholar."

CAPTAIN WILLIAM WHIPPLE (1695 - 1751)

William Whipple came from Ipswich, MA, married Mary, the daughter of Robert Cutt, and settled in Kittery. They lived in the Cutt-Whipple garrison house on Locke's Cove. Born in this same house, their second son, **William** (1730-1785), was brought up in Portsmouth. Mariner, sea captain, merchant and a representative to Congress in 1776, this William Whipple was one of the three signers of the Declaration of Independence from New Hampshire.

THE PEPPERRELL FAMILY

The first **William Pepperrell** came from Devonshire, England. Born in 1646, he was hoping to make his fortune in the new world and settled on the Isles of Shoals to cure and market fish. He married Margery, the daughter of **John Bray** of Kittery, and in 1682 at the age of 36, he built a house on a part of his father-in-law's land in Kittery Point. Here he became a very successful merchant and trader with many fishing and trading ships traveling throughout the West Indies and to Europe. It was said that he was the richest man in New England and the truly handsome house he built stands today on the left of Frisbee's Market. An early leader of Kittery, he served as justice of the peace, commander of Fort William (today known as Fort McClary), captain of the militia, eventually rising to the rank of lieutenant-colonel. One of the founders of the Congregational Church in Kittery Point, he died in 1734 and was buried in the orchard near his house, now marked by a marble tomb brought from England. His wife, Margery, died about seven years later.

The first William Pepperrell's second son, who came to be known as **Sir William Pepperrell**, was born in 1696 in Kittery Point and had an elementary education. However, he learned a great deal from his father about business, sailing a ship, writing and keeping records and, most important, how to manage men. He continued his father's trade in fish, lumber and West India goods and became wealthy in his own right. In 1723, age 27, he married Mary Hirst of Boston. At 30, he held the rank of colonel in the militia and was appointed to the Governor's Council. The people of Kittery elected him their representative in 1726-1727 and by 1730 he held the office of chief justice.

In 1745, during the French and Indian Wars, Pepperrell commanded a force of three or four thousand men, mostly from Maine, against the French fortress of Louisburg on Cape Breton Island (now Nova Scotia). He contributed five thousand dollars of his own money to this daring campaign. After a six-week siege, Pepperrell's British forces were victorious over the French and he was hailed a hero. In London, William Pepperrell became the first American-born baronet created by King George II. He died at 63, in 1759, and is buried with his father in Kittery Point.

MARY HIRST, LADY PEPPERRELL (CIRCA **1708 -1789**)
Six years after the death of her husband, **Lady Pepperrell** built an elegant home in the Georgian style, close to the Congregational Church in Kittery Point, living there until her death in 1789. After the Revolutionary War, all the Pepperrell property was confiscated by the new government because of their loyalist sympathies.

JOHN BRAY (CIRCA **1620** – CIRCA **1690**)
John Bray probably built his house in 1662. It is the oldest house in Kittery Point, and reputedly the oldest in the state of Maine, as well. In 1672, it operated as a public house. Along with William Pepperrell, Nicholas Frost, and Alexander Shapleigh, John Bray also came from Devonshire, England.

JOHN HALEY BELLAMY (1836 – 1914)
Born in 1836, **John Bellamy** is one of Kittery's best known native sons. Bellamy was a wood carver of hanging wall eagles. From the 1850s on, he was recognized for his creativity and originality and has been often copied. He also carved clock cases, furniture,

animal figures, stern boards and signs. His most famous sculpture is the monumental eagle figure head created for the **USS LANCASTER** in Portsmouth in the late 1870s. This gilded masterpiece weighs 3,200 pounds, and boasts a wingspan of eighteen feet. It is now on permanent display at the Mariners' Museum in Newport News, Virginia.

The Bellamy eagle figure head from the USS LANCASTER.

HORACE MITCHELL

Born in 1857 in Kittery, **Horace Mitchell** came from a long line of first settlers. Originally a teacher, he later worked as a clerk in the Marshall House Hotel in York Harbor and then at the Wentworth Hotel in New Castle, NH. From 1885 to 1890, he worked at the Pocahontas Hotel on Gerrish Island, and in 1890, built the Champernowne Hotel at the end of Lawrence Lane in Kittery Point, which burned to the ground after World War I. Representing Kittery in 1891 in the state government, by 1895 he had been elected a state senator. He was postmaster in Kittery Point until 1897 and a devoted Mason. The Mitchell Primary School in Kittery Point is named after him.

THE ISLES OF SHOALS

The history of the **Isles of Shoals** is tied closely with that of Kittery. Several mainland settlers first lived on and fished from the Isles. At the height of the Isles' prosperity in the mid 1600s, about 500 men lived on the islands. As the fishing grounds declined, so did the population. By the time of the Revolutionary War, all residents were ordered off so there would be no temptation to aid the enemy. The Isles enjoyed a revival in the mid to late 1800s with the great resort hotel movement. Maine owns five of the islands (within Kittery's jurisdiction) while New Hampshire owns the remaining four. Today, it is a quieter scene with a harbor, conference center and a marine laboratory on the various islands. See page **23**.

During the 1800s, the railroads, resort hotels and the shipyard were pivotal in the development of Kittery. You will find more about these topics as you read this guide.

Students of an earlier time sit on the steps of the Austin School.

EARLY HISTORY

SOURCES:

Charles Penrose, *Old Kittery, Land of Adventure 1647 and Captain Francis Champernowne (1614-1687)*. New York: Newcomen Society of England, American Branch, 1947.

Everett S. Stackpole, *Old Kittery and Her Families*. Lewiston, ME: Press of Lewiston Journal Company, 1903.

Cecil Hampden Cutts Howard, *Genealogy of the Cutts Family in America*. 1892.

Louise Dickinson Rich, *The Coast of Maine, An Informal History and Guide*. Camden, ME: Down East Books, 1975.

Lyman V. Rutledge, *Ten Miles Out: Guide Book to The Isles of Shoals*. Boston, MA: Isles of Shoals Association, 1972.

Sir John Bernard Burke, *Burke's American Families with British Ancestry*. Genealogical Publishing Co., 1996.

Edmund Charles Tarbell, II, *William Badger (1752-1830) Master Shipbuilder of Maine*. Newcomen Society, 1955.

Yvonne Brault Smith, *John Haley Bellamy, Carver of Eagles*. Portsmouth, NH: Peter E. Randall, Publisher, 1982.

Victor Stafford, *John Haley Bellamy, The Woodcarver of Kittery Point*. *Antiques* magazine, 1935.

Kittery Historical and Naval Museum, *Ancient and Modern Kittery, The Gateway To Maine: The Oldest Incorporated Township in the State*. 1986.

Kittery Bicentennial Committee, *Kittery Kaleidoscope, 1976*. Somersworth, NH: NH Printers, 1976.

300th Anniversary Publication Committee, *Old Kittery, 1647-1947*. Kittery, ME: Piscataqua Press, 1947.

Kittery Community Service Association, *Kittery, Ancient and Modern*. Kittery, ME: 1925.

1999 Update of the Kittery Comprehensive Plan. Kittery, ME: 1999.

WEBSITES:

www.SeacoastNH.com; www.en.wikipedia.org; www.kittery.org

SHORT HISTORY OF THE
PORTSMOUTH NAVAL SHIPYARD

Kittery has always taken great pride in the Portsmouth Naval Shipyard and we hope in the following chapter to share this pride with you.

EARLY HISTORY OF THE HARBOR
Kittery has been the home to shipbuilding since the 1600s. Martin Pring, an Englishman, was the first European to explore the Piscataqua River in 1603. Next came Samuel de Champlain in 1605, followed by Captain John Smith in 1615. However it was Sir Ferdinando Gorges who actually received a grant of land from King Charles I of England, in 1639.

The Kittery/Portsmouth shores were a natural place to build ships for many reasons. The exceptionally swift Piscataqua River does not freeze in winter and many islands at the river's mouth were close to the open ocean. Masts and bowsprits for sailing ships needed the tallest and straightest trees, which were abundantly supplied by the New World's virgin forests, as was lumber of all kinds for the rest of the ships.

By 1690, the British Royal Navy had a contract to build in this port. **HMS FALKLAND**, a 637-ton frigate of 54 guns, was the first British warship to be built in North America. **HMS BEDFORD**, carrying 32 guns, was completed in 1697 and **HMS AMERICA**, 60 guns, was launched in 1749. And so the Kittery shipbuilding tradition began. Master carpenters, gunsmiths, ammunition experts, sail makers, ironmongers, accountants and naval designers were drawm to this part of the world to make their living.

THE REVOLUTIONARY WAR

To protect this valuable harbor, the British built Fort William & Mary (now Fort Constitution) in New Castle, NH, in the late 1600s. In the dead of winter, December 14 and 15, 1774, a group of patriots from Kittery and Portsmouth captured the fort and brought down the British flag. This is thought to be the first act of aggression against the British Crown in America. The ammunition and supplies that were captured were hidden in the countryside, later to be used against the British, at Lexington and Concord on April 19, 1775, and at the battle at Bunker Hill on June 17 of the same year.

With the outbreak of war, shipbuilding became even more important to the region. In 1775, the Continental Congress authorized thirteen new frigates to be built; in 1776, the **USS RALEIGH**, a 32-gun frigate was launched from a boatyard in Portsmouth.

A year later, the **USS RANGER** was built on Badger's Island for John Paul Jones. Commissioned in 1777, the 18-gun sloop was the first man-of-war to fly the new American flag and received the first official salute from a foreign nation, France, in 1778. **RANGER** captured many prize ships from 1778 to 1780 but was captured herself in 1780 by the British in Charleston, South Carolina.

John Paul Jones, "Father of the American Navy."

PORTSMOUTH NAVAL SHIPYARD ESTABLISHED

For the same reasons that the British chose to build their ships in Kittery, the new Secretary of the Navy, Benjamin Stoddard, recommended to President Jefferson that a permanent Navy shipyard be established there. Land was purchased in June, 1800. The name, **Portsmouth Naval Shipyard,** was chosen because in 1800 Maine was not yet a state. (Maine joined the Union in 1820.) Kittery, a part of Massachusetts at that time, had no post office and so the name Portsmouth, which did have a post office, was used for the new shipyard. Throughout the 20th century, primarily because both states wanted to collect taxes, there was disagreement as to which state claimed jurisdiction over the Shipyard. This was finally settled on May 29, 2001, when the US Supreme Court handed down a ruling that the Shipyard was, indeed, in Maine. The Portsmouth Naval Shipyard is the oldest continuously operated shipyard in this country.

WAR OF 1812

At the beginning of the War of 1812 against Great Britain, the United States Navy was only twenty years old and, in March of 1812, had only three ships in the Shipyard undergoing minor overhauls, the **USS WASP**, a sloop of war, the **USS RATTLESNAKE**, a schooner, and the **USS ENTERPRISE**, a brig. In contrast, as the War of 1812 broke out, the British Navy, the most powerful in the world at that time, had 97 ships in American waters.

A Navy barber plies his trade on the USS ENTERPRISE, early in the 19th century.

HISTORY 📖

Commodore Isaac Hull was appointed the first Commandant of the Shipyard in February 1813. In 1814, the keel was laid for the first ship to be built at the Portsmouth Naval Shipyard, the **USS WASHINGTON**, a 74-gun ship of the line. It was terribly hard to get materials because of the British blockade of the harbor. In response, the Shipyard began designing and making their own marine hardware. The war ended with the signing of the Treaty of Ghent (Belgium) in December of 1814.

By 1822, a bridge was completed between Portsmouth and Kittery. Before the bridge, all the workmen at the Shipyard took the ferry or rowed themselves. In 1827, President John Quincy Adams, in accordance with an Act of Congress, drew up a comprehensive plan for the future development of the Shipyard.

FROM SAIL TO STEAM

In 1843, one of the last naval sailing ships constructed at the Shipyard was the **USS PORTSMOUTH**, a 24-gun sloop of war, designed by master builder Josiah Baker, and her beauty was widely noted. In 1847 the first steamer was built at the Shipyard, a side wheel steam frigate named the **USS SARANAC**. The entire workforce of 143 men took part in her construction.

To facilitate construction and repair of naval vessels, a floating dry dock and basin was deemed necessary. In 1851, construction began on the Floating Balance Dry Dock and Marine Railway. The dry dock itself was built on Peirce Island, opposite the Shipyard, then floated across the river. The US Navy's *Cradle of American Shipbuilding* gives a detailed description of this amazing apparatus:

> It was 350 feet long and 105'-4" wide outside, and with walls 38 feet high. The wall on each side was 7'-8" wide. On each wall there was an engine and boiler of 50 horsepower geared and connected with 12 pumps. These pumps raised seventeen thousand, four hundred and eighteen tons of water per hour and were capable of raising a ship of 5000 tons.

The use of a hydraulic engine operated by steam made Portsmouth the most efficient shipyard on the Atlantic. The second steamship and first screw steamer, the **USS MOHICAN**, was launched in 1857.

THE CIVIL WAR

Everyone at the Shipyard knew by 1861 that war was inevitable. All officers (commissioned, warrant and civil), clerks, master workmen, mechanics, laborers, lodge men and marines had to take the oath of allegiance to the United States, which was administered by the Commandant of the Shipyard.

The keels of the **USS OSSIPEE** and the **USS KEARSARGE** were laid in 1861, both 9 gun steam sloops of war. The more famous **KEARSARGE** defeated the notorious Confederate raider **CSS ALABAMA** off the coast of Cherbourg, France. **ALABAMA,** whose defeat came on June 21, 1864, had burned 57 Union ships besides capturing and releasing many others.

By 1862, the Shipyard was now employing 2000 men and everyone was working at full capacity. A total of 26 ships were built during this period, 18 steam sloops and 2 ironclads, the **USS PASSACONAWAY** and **USS AGAMENTICUS.** Admiral David G. Farragut, famous for his blockade of New Orleans at the start of the Civil War and the capture and blockade of Mobile Bay at the end of the war, died at the Portsmouth Naval Shipyard on August 14, 1870. His flagship, **USS FRANKLIN** was the largest vessel launched on the Piscataqua River at that time.

SPANISH AMERICAN WAR

The Spanish American War was fought by the United States against Spain, who in 1898 held the island of Cuba. In July of 1898, the Shipyard began building a prison stockade for 1200 Spanish prisoners known as Camp Long. Built on the south end of Seavey Island, it was the future home of the now decommissioned Naval Prison.

Noted author and editor of the *Atlantic Monthly,* William Dean Howells, a summer resident of Kittery Point, writes of a visit to the stockade to watch the prisoners put on a mock bull fight in his *Confessions of a Summer Colonist,* published in 1900:

> The toro (bull) himself was composed of two prisoners, whose horizontal backs were covered with a brown blanket; and his feet sometimes bare and sometimes shod with India-rubber boots were of the human parts. I stayed to see three bulls killed; the last was uncommonly fierce, and when his hindquarters came off or out, his forequarters charged joyously among the aficionados on the prisoners side, and made havoc in the thickly packed ranks.

HISTORY 📖

Spanish prisoners, 1898.

By 1899 change and expansion at the Shipyard resulted in the first telephone service and electric lighting. Construction of the main building of the Naval Prison began in 1903 and was finished in 1908.

On July 22, 1905, Henderson's Point, referred to more colorfully by locals as "Pull-or-be-Damned Point," was blown to smithereens. In this extraordinary feat of naval engineering, 46 tons of dynamite were used to shear seventy thousand tons of rock from the south end of Seavey Island. The enormous blast at Henderson Point, the single largest explosion ever attempted anywhere up to that time, brought worldwide attention to Portsmouth.

The explosion of Henderson Point.

RUSSO - JAPANESE PEACE TREATY

In 1905 President Theodore Roosevelt brought another kind of world attention to the Portsmouth Naval Shipyard. At the President's invitation, envoys from Russia and Japan met at the Shipyard to discuss terms for ending a two-year war between these powers over Korea and Manchuria. It was not a foregone conclusion that they would reach a compromise, but on September 5, 1905, after a month of multi-track negotiations, they did. The Treaty of Portsmouth was signed in Building #86 at the Portsmouth Naval Shipyard.

WORLD WAR I AND THE AGE OF SUBMARINES

August 1914 marked the beginning of World War I. With the sinking of **RMS LUSITANIA** by a German submarine in 1915, subs began to play an important role in the US Navy. The Portsmouth Naval Shipyard was chosen to build the first American submarine; the keel was promptly laid for the L-8 that year. Completed in 1917, she took her place as the first in a long line of Portsmouth-built submarines. By 1923 the Shipyard was officially designated as a submarine yard.

With young men joining the military services nationwide, one notable side effect of America's entrance into the World War was a serious drain of workers at the Shipyard. A night school, designed to improve the skills of men already at the Shipyard, grew rapidly and was so successful that an apprentice program was started and

Early 20th century traffic on the bridge to the Yard.

PORTSMOUTH NAVAL SHIPYARD

continues to graduate skilled workers today. The Shipyard expanded from fewer than 2000 workers at the start of the war to 5722 by 1918, with a workforce that included over 1000 women. At this time the Shipyard also became an electrical manufacturing plant, producing excellent high-quality, low-cost fittings and fixtures for every kind of ship in the Navy. Five submarines were completed by 1923, and five Fleet type V class submarines were built by 1929. They remained part of our fleet in 1945.

On the tragic day of May 23, 1939, the **USS SQUALUS** sank off the Isles of Shoals with a crew of 59 aboard. She was on sea trials in 240 feet of water when her main induction valve failed to close.

The launching of the USS SQUALUS.

USS SCULPIN, sister ship to the SQUALUS, located the stricken sub, and rescue vessels and workers converged on the scene from Boston, New London, and Washington. The McCann rescue chamber, an experimental diving bell, was rushed to the spot, and over the next day and a half, 33 survivors were brought to the surface. After a heroic struggle, the **USS SQUALUS** was finally raised on September 13 and towed to the Shipyard.

The **SQUALUS** was decommissioned, rebuilt and recommissioned as the **USS SAILFISH** the following year, and went on to distinguish herself with an excellent record in the Second World War. The bridge and conning tower of the **SAILFISH**, located today on the mall of the Shipyard, serve as a memorial to the 26 brave officers, enlisted men and civilians lost on the **SQUALUS**.

HISTORY

PORTSMOUTH NAVAL SHIPYARD

WORLD WAR II
Almost half of all the submarines that took part in the Second World War were built at the Portsmouth Naval Shipyard.

The **USS SNAPPER,** commissioned in 1937, was the first all-welded submarine. Stronger hull construction made it possible for subs to submerge to deeper water and to better withstand depth bombing attacks. By the end of 1941, an active mine field was laid at the entrance to Portsmouth Harbor and an anti-submarine net installed from Fort Foster, in Kittery Point, to Fort Stark in New Castle, NH, to prevent German submarines entering the harbor.

The USS SNAPPER in dry dock.

After December 7, 1941, and the outbreak of war, the Shipyard initiated an intense building program, constructing over 104 submarines by the end of 1943; 32 submarines were completed in 1944 alone. By 1944, the Shipyard employed 20,466 workers, a record number, many of whom were women. On January 27, 1944, four submarines were launched on the same day. The Portsmouth Naval Shipyard was the largest submarine base on the Atlantic Coast and was well placed to receive the surrender of German submarines captured in North Atlantic waters.

A German officer surrenders to authorities at the Portsmouth Naval Shipyard, May 19, 1945.

MOVING TOWARD THE NUCLEAR AGE

Studying tactics and casualty rates in the U S Navy after the war led to a new era of submarine construction.

The importance of increased submergence time and depth, higher underwater speed, silent operations and better listening equipment marked the beginning of the GUPPY program (GUPPY standing for Greater Underwater Propulsion Power - the Y was added for sound effects). With this program, all deck fittings were removed, recessed or streamlined, and the conning tower and periscope enclosed within the "sail" area. Again the Portsmouth Naval Shipyard designers, construction men and women were ahead of the curve, reaching out into new horizons in hydrodynamics, sonics and nucleonics.

With our engagement in the Korean War, 1951, **USS TANG,** the first fast attack prototype, was commissioned. This SS563 class sub included great improvements in higher submerged speed, firepower, torpedo firing, superior sonar and radar detection and increased submerged depth.

By 1953, the Shipyard produced the **USS ALBACORE** (SS569), a truly dramatic advance in design. This experimental submarine was reputedly the fastest and most maneuverable ship of her time. She is now on permanent display in Portsmouth and available for tours of inspection. (Albacore Museum, 600 Market Street, Portsmouth, N H. 603-436-3680.)

USS ALBACORE, launched August 1, 1953.

On January 25, 1956, the keel of the nuclear powered **USS SWORDFISH** was laid and she was commissioned in September of 1958. A sister ship, **USS SEA DRAGON,** was completed by December 1959. **SEA DRAGON** was the first ship to cross under the North Pole from Atlantic to Pacific, the famed Northwest Passage.

In 1959, designers realized the need for a sound basin to measure and analyze underwater noises and to be able to take corrective action. An Acoustical Radiation Measurement Basin was constructed between Clark Island and Jamaica Island and is the only such sound survey facility within a Naval facility. Because the Portsmouth

Naval Shipyard has pioneered the development of instruments for measuring noise, the US Navy has the quietest submarines in the world today. The **USS ABRAHAM LINCOLN**, completed in 1961, was the first Polaris missile submarine built at the Shipyard.

The Shipyard's first Polaris missile submarine, the USS ABRAHAM LINCOLN.

The **USS THRESHER**, designed and built at the Portsmouth Naval Shipyard and launched in 1960, was a nuclear attack submarine, deep diving and quieter than others. Her tear-drop shaped hull, like the **ALBACORE**, gave her greater underwater speed, and she had the most advanced, state-of-the-art integrated sensor and weapons systems yet launched. On April 9, 1963, during sea trials, she submerged with 129 men, never to resurface. With the **USS THRESHER** disaster, the Navy learned many painful lessons, among them, depth limitations on all deep-diving submarines and safety improvements in the construction of all new submarines.

On September 25, 1971, **USS SAND LANCE,** a Sturgeon-class Cold War "ship of the line" of the attack fleet, was the 134th and last submarine to be lauched from the Portsmouth Naval Shipyard.

TO THE PRESENT TIME
From the 1980's, BRAC (Base Realignment and Closure) has been a constant threat to the Portsmouth Naval Shipyard. So far the Shipyard has survived, primarily for nuclear submarine overhaul

and repair work. It also supports nuclear submarines throughout their full life cycle.

A submarine crew on deck.

For the past 205 years, in wartime and in peace, the Portsmouth Naval Shipyard has always reached for the highest standards and scientific breakthroughs. They established the use of life buoys, the Momsen Lung, the McCann Submarine Rescue Chamber, the submarine test tank and the PERA program (Planning & Engineering for Repairs & Alterations). This is why we are so proud of our Shipyard.

Unfortunately, the Portsmouth Naval Shipyard is not open to the public.

Some information contained in this chapter was obtained from the U. S. Government. However, this Guidebook does not represent official U. S. Government information, and does not represent the views or positions of the U. S. Government or the Portsmouth Naval Shipyard.

SOURCES:
United States Navy, **Cradle of American Shipbuilding**, 1971. (Publication of the Portsmouth Naval Shipyard)
W. Jeffrey Bolster, Editor, **Cross-Grained & Wily Waters**, 2002.

WEBSITES:
www.SeacoastNH.com; www.en.wikipedia.org; www.nps.gov.

ISLES OF SHOALS

The Isles of Shoals are a group of nine islands roughly ten miles out from Portsmouth harbor. On a sunny day they are clearly visible from Fort Foster (see page **47**). In fact, the Isles are piles of granite rock tossed up in the last Ice Age. The islands have a thin coating of top-soil and can sustain scrub grass and huckleberry bushes. They are ringed by rocky outcroppings of sharp boulders, bleached from years of salt spray and crashing waves.

> These islands have a dreary and inhospitable appearance, and but for their advantageous situation for carrying on the fisheries, would probably have never been inhabited. They are a bed of rocks, raising their disjointed heads above the water.
>
> Rev. Jedediah Morse
> *Description of the Isles of Shoals*, 1800

These nine islands are surrounded by ledges. Some say the water racing over these shallow rocks gave the islands their name but others claim that the name comes from the "shoaling" or "schooling" of fish that were in great abundance in these waters. Four hundred years ago the first recorded explorers came to these islands and discovered great quantities of fish.

A dividing line through the middle of Gosport Harbor, bordered by Smuttynose, Cedar and Star Islands, marks the boundary between New Hampshire and Maine. Both states wanted to own the rich fishing grounds of the Shoals; this state line gives the five northern islands: Hog (later named Appledore), Duck, Cedar, Malaga, and Smuttynose to Maine (all under the jurisdiction of Kittery). The four southern islands:

Star, Lunging (sometimes called Londoners), Seavey and White, are in New Hampshire.

EUROPEAN DISCOVERY

In 1603, Martin Pring and his ship the **SPEEDWELL** passed by these Islands on the way up the Piscataqua River. He was looking for timber, furs and sassafras which was thought to be a cure for the French Pox (syphilis). In 1614, Captain John Smith was sent to the New World by the London Company. He named the islands **"Smyth's Isles"** and described them in his writings, *Description of New England, 1616,* but the name did not stick.

As there were no Indians on the Islands, the first inhabitants were most probably sailors and fishermen who came for the catch. Only about one-third of a ship's company of men lived on shore, the rest lived on board their ships, as it was more important to use the land for drying the fish. The dried cod, called dunfish, produced on the Shoals actually set the world market price, as it sold for three to four times the amount of dried cod produced in other regions. The old Mediterranean coins found on the Isles are a result of foreign shipwrecks in the treacherous water surrounding the Isles. The ships from Mediterranean countries were at the Shoals in search of dunfish, called *baccala* in their home countries.

Mackerel, cod, haddock, and mullet were caught, de-headed and gutted, then salted before they were laid on racks or drying flakes for three or four weeks. Then the dried fish were packed up and returned to feed the people in Europe.

Richard Cutt and his brothers came to the Shoals from Wales in 1646 and started a successful fishing business before moving to the mainland. Two went to Portsmouth and the third, Robert, came to Kittery. William Pepperrell had settled on Hog (later named Appledore) Island by 1676, and he too did very well before resettling in Kittery (see page **4**).

But these successful men were largely exceptions. Most Shoals fishermen eked out a living by leasing their equipment from others. It was a very hard life. By the mid 1650s there were at least two taverns and a meetinghouse at the Shoals. The town of Gosport on Star Island was established in 1715 and named after

an English village not far from Portsmouth, England. The Rev. John Tucke, who came to the Shoals in 1730, was ordained in the Gosport meetinghouse and ministered to the Shoalers for the next 40 years. His arrival marked the point when the first Gosport town records began. Tucke also acted as the magistrate and physician on Star Island. The Shoalers often paid him in fish. John Tucke died in 1773.

REVOLUTIONARY WAR
During the Revolutionary War, the Shoals were evacuated, both for the Shoalers' own protection, and, some suspect, because of their independent nature; there was fear that the locals would interact with the British. Many of the more successful and respected families moved to Portsmouth or Kittery, some floating their homes to the mainland on barges (page **75**). After the Revolutionary War the population of the islands declined. In 1800, only a handful of families lived on the islands.

THE WHITE ISLAND LIGHT
In 1839, Thomas Laighton arrived as lighthouse keeper on White Island with his wife, daughter Celia, age 4, and infant son Oscar, 3 months old. Laighton came from a prominent Portsmouth, NH, family. He was assistant postmaster and served in the Custom House. A capable man and an entrepreneur, he formed a working men's reading club, co-founded the Portsmouth Whaling Company and co-edited the *New Hampshire Gazette*. In 1837, he was elected to the State Legislature. Laighton and his brother bought Hog, Smuttynose, Malaga and Cedar islands in 1839 with the hope of reviving the fishing industry at the Shoals.

By 1840 another son, Cedric, was born and in 1841, this family of five moved to the Mid-Atlantic, a boarding house/hotel on Smuttynose Island, owned by Samuel Haley. Eliza Laighton, Thomas' wife, ran the hotel to earn extra income for the family while he was serving in the state legislature. She was known as a very congenial hostess and her fish chowder was renowned. The Laightons' success with this venture most likely contributed to Thomas' idea of building a resort hotel on Appledore.

The nineteenth century was one of great expansion of trade all over the country. Goods were transported by ship and the shipping

ISLES OF SHOALS

lanes were busy around the Shoals and Portsmouth/Kittery harbors. Knowledge of sailing was very important and the only method of getting around for the people of the Shoals was by boat.

By the middle of the 19th century, seven fishermen, their wives and families lived on Star Island, while 80 sheep, 3 cows and plenty of chickens roamed on Hog Island. Once a week a Reverend Plummer held services at the stone church on Star Island and Mrs. Laighton made an annual trip to Portsmouth for supplies.

The Stone Church, Isles of Shoals, built in 1800.

THE HOTEL ERA

After seven years as lighthouse keeper, Thomas Laighton built a house on Hog Island, moved his family again and began plans for a summer hotel. Levi Thaxter, a young man who had studied law at Harvard, became his partner. Thaxter had visited the Laightons on White Island and had returned for several winters to teach the three Laighton children.

Appledore House, on the Isles of Shoals.

The hotel partners changed the name of the island from Hog to Appledore and named their hotel Appledore House. Opening on June 15, 1848, Appledore House proved to be a great success. There were many literary visitors to Appledore House, including Nathaniel Hawthorne, Franklin Pierce (who would later be addressed as President Pierce) and Richard Henry Dana, author of *Two Years before the Mast*.

CELIA THAXTER

Over the years Levi Thaxter had fallen in love with Celia Laighton and in 1851, when Celia was 16 and Levi 27, they were married in the parlor of Appledore House.

The Thaxters moved to Newtonville, Massachusetts, near the Charles River. Celia was grateful for the life she had, but longed for the open water of the Shoals. She expressed this yearning in a poem, *"Landlocked,"* that was submitted anonymously to Boston's *Atlantic Monthly* magazine. Its publication launched Celia's writing career. Her most famous poem is entitled *"Sandpiper."*

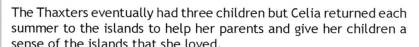

ISLES OF SHOALS

The Thaxters eventually had three children but Celia returned each summer to the islands to help her parents and give her children a sense of the islands that she loved.

In 1873, Celia's book, *Among the Isles of Shoals,* was published to good reviews and much praise. Due to her writing and Levi's Boston connections, Celia became part of an informal literary group which visited her on Appledore. Writers such as William Dean Howells, Sarah Orne Jewett, James Russell Lowell and John Greenleaf Whittier, and artists including Childe Hassam, J. Appleton Brown, Ross Turner and William Morris Hunt came to work and enjoy good company and conversation. Childe Hassam painted a number of luminous paintings here, in what would later be termed his American Impressionist style.

In 1873, two infamous murders were committed on Smuttynose Island. An extended family, consisting of three men and three women, were the only inhabitants of Smuttynose at the time. One night in Portsmouth, the three men encountered Louis Wagner, a Prussian who had stayed with them the summer before. It's speculated that Wagner realized that the women were alone back on Smuttynose and that there was money in their house. Wagner is said to have rowed the ten miles out to Smuttynose, surprised the women, killed two of them (one was strangled and the other killed with an ax) and then rowed back to Portsmouth. The third woman, in her nightgown and barefoot, fled to the rocks carrying her small dog. She survived, was rescued the following morning and accused Louis Wagner of having commited the deed. Celia Thaxter later wrote about the murders in her 1875 essay for the *Atlantic Monthly,* "Memorable Murder."

Celia Thaxter died in 1899 at the age of 59. After the decline of the resort era at the Isles of Shoals, Appledore House burned down to the ground in 1914.

TODAY AT THE ISLES
In the 1870's another "grand hotel," the Oceanic, opened on Star Island. It burned down two years later but was quickly rebuilt and prospered for many years. In 1897, a group of Unitarians began holding summer conferences at the Oceanic Hotel. Later, the Star Island Corporation was formed to buy Star Island and today still

operates religious retreats for adults, teens and families with children during the summer months. Information about the Star Island conferences can be found at http://www.starisland.org. Today the religious organizations that operate the conferences are Unitarian, Universalist and Congregationalist.

The Oceanic Hotel.

Today, as we enter the twenty-first century, the Isles of Shoals are returning to their sparse beauty. The Shoals Marine Laboratory now leases Appledore Island and operates the largest undergraduate facility of its kind in North America to study marine ecology, geology, climates and marine law.

Under the auspices of Cornell University and the University of New Hampshire, the Shoals Marine Lab sponsors over 20 summer credit courses where students come and live for 10 weeks and study ecology and the environment. For more information, contact Laurie Johnson, Cornell's Admissions Counselor, (607) 255-0743 or LHJ1@cornell.edu, or visit the Shoals Marine Lab website at: http://www.sml.cornell.edu.

The Shoals Marine Lab also has a Bird Banding Program to study the migration stop-over ecology of over 130 species of birds. This Banding Station is operated by volunteers. If you wish to learn more, contact morriss@gort.canisius.edu, or pay a visit to their website: http://www.sml.cornell.edu/research/prbbp.htm.

ISLES OF SHOALS

SOURCES:
A Stern and Lovely Scene: A Visual History of the Isles of Shoals.
University Art Galleries, University of New Hampshire, (Durham, New Hampshire 1978).
Gosport Remembered, The Last Village of the Isles of Shoals. edited by Peter E. Randall and Maryellen Burke, (Portsmouth, N H: Portsmouth Marine Society, 1997).
Cross-Grained & Wily Waters: A Guide to the Piscataqua Maritime Region. Editor, W. Jeffrey Bolster. Portsmouth, NH: Peter E. Randall Publisher, 2002.
Ninety Years at the Isles of Shoals, by Oscar Laighton. Andover, MA: The Andover Press, 1929.

WEBSITES:
www.SeacoastNH.com; www.starisland.org; www.sml.cornell.edu; www.nsf.gov/home/crssprgm/reu/

Haley Cottage, on the Isles of Shoals.

TRAINS, TROLLEYS & RESORT HOTELS

The "golden spike" was driven into the rail bed on May 10, 1869, in Promontory Summit, Utah, instantly connecting the East coast with the West coast. This was a giant leap for the United States, joining it forever as one nation. Inevitably the railroad, during the 1870's and 1880's, spread its spidery rails throughout New England, bringing with it increased commerce and prosperity.

YORK HARBOR AND BEACH RAILWAY
By 1887, the **York Harbor and Beach Railway** began freight and passenger service to this area. With locomotives powered by steam, its route paralleled today's Route 103, from Kittery Junction, Kittery Navy Yard, and on to Kittery Point at the end of Coleman Avenue. The route continued through Bedell, Oakland Farm, Seabury, York Harbor, Long Beach and Ocean Side, and terminated in York Beach.

YORK HARBOR AND BEACH RAILROAD CO.

JULY 1, 1923

Miles	Svcs	STATION	State	Jct.	X-ref
0.00	T-P	Kittery Jct.	Me.	Port. Div.	12
0.93	TFP	Kittery Navy Yard			
2.80	TFP	Kittery Point			
4.76	---	Bedell			
5.52	---	Oakland Farm			
6.82	--P	Seabury (Summer Sta.)			
8.12	TFP	York Harbor			
9.33		Long Beach (Summer Sta.)			
10.20		Ocean Side (Summer Sta.)			
10.98	TFP	York Beach			

Svcs: T=Telegraph, F=Freight Accounts, P=Ticket Accounts

A vintage York Harbor and Beach Railroad schedule.

By connecting to other lines, this train line forged a new link between Kittery and the distant city of Boston and beyond. Many men could now commute to jobs in Boston.

As Rosamund Thaxter, Celia Thaxter's great-niece, recalls in her memoirs, *Aunt Rozzie Remembers*:

> The old railroad station at Kittery Point was located down what is now Coleman Avenue. Here all the men gathered who were going on the Boston & Maine trains. There was an old pot-bellied stove good to spit at, and a ticket office. In later years the steam train from York Beach came puffing along, having first stopped at York Harbor and York Village before going on to the Navy Yard and Portsmouth. There were about four trains a day.

Ten years later, in 1897, the **Portsmouth, Kittery and York Street Railway** was started by the Atlantic Shore Line Railway Company. Also known as the **Electric Railroad**, PK&Y proposed opening trolley service in direct competition with the **York Harbor & Beach Railway.** For the eleven months preceeding the PK&Y's inauguraal trip on August 12, 1897, furious editorials in the *York Courant* newspaper opposed this enterprise.

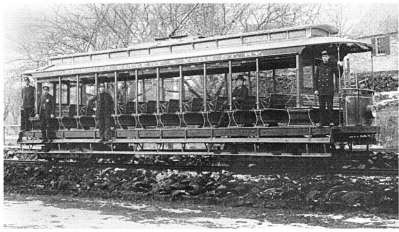

A PK&Y trolley.

York Harbor residents, in particular, opposed the new service; their summer hotels were older and firmly established, and they expressed concern that the PK&Y would bring "riff raff" into the rather aristocratic company of York Harbor. In April of that year, an editorial in the *Courant* proclaimed:

> York is head and shoulders ahead of Kittery Point in growth and prosperity as a summer resort. Any Selectman of York who is afraid to block this Kittery Point scheme is a traitor to York's interest and to the public sentiment of York.

Scheme or not, it was just good business sense for Kittery Point to push for the electric rail service. Two hotel proprietors, Horace Mitchell of the **Champernowne** and Samuel Jennison of the **Pocahontas**, were directors of the company. They hoped to offer convenience for the people of Kittery as well as jobs and a delightful excursion for their summer visitors.

The PK&Y line included a steam ferry service across the Piscataqua River on boats large enough to take on teams of horses and trolley cars. The **KITTERY** and the **ALICE HOWARD** plied the swift waters of the Piscataqua, docking at the ferry slip on Badger's Island where the warmth of a heated station awaited them. A steam plant in Kittery Point provided the power supply (electricity was relatively inexpensive at the time) with direct current; dispatching was handled by telephone to the car-houses, substations and booths placed at the train turnouts. This was very modern!

The PK&Y Power Station, Kittery Point.

The PK&Y road bed was crooked but picturesque as it followed the shore. It needed many trestles to cross the creeks, coves and harbors along the route. The longest trestle, crossing Brave Boat Harbor, was nearly a quarter of a mile long, and its remains are all that one can see today of the tracks.

Remains of trolley trestles, mute sentinels of a by-gone era, still stand in Brave Boat Harbor today.

The PK&Y went into operation on August 27, 1897, with a fare of 2 cents a mile, 5 cents between stops or 25 cents for the whole trip of 15½ miles. It was about an hour and a half ride of pure joy on a warm summer day. The PK&Y was one of the first trolley companies to operate a post office car.

A variety of styles of trolley cars served Kittery passengers. In winter, an enclosed, plush 28-seat car, with coal-burning boilers that provided hot water heat, was a welcome sight. (By 1918, the trolleys were heated by electric heat.) In summer, a 4-wheeled, 14-bench, 70-passenger open car popularly known as "a breezer" was very popular. Trolleys were run by a two-man crew. The conductor was in charge and collected fares. The motorman operated the trolley, activating the vehicle's hand brake by turning a brass "gooseneck" handle.

After the initial opposition, the PK&Y settled in to become a great convenience to all the inhabitants. Children went to school on the

trolley, and men and women used it to commute to Portsmouth and to the Navy Yard. In winter, the tracks were cleared promptly of snow. Again, from *Aunt Rozzie Remembers:*

> I remember the breezy summer day when cousin Betty and I were making our weekly expedition to York Harbor to take our drawing lessons with Miss Susan Ricker Knox. Betty lost her straw hat! It blew off, sailed through the air for a bit, but conveniently came to rest on the dry marsh a few feet from the incoming tide. A shriek from the little ten-year-old girls made the motorman, who knew us well, slam on his brakes. He somehow climbed down and rescued the brown Tyrolean straw hat with its bright wreath of buttercups, much to the amusement of the other passengers.

Both year-round inhabitants and summer visitors relied on this service for local transportation, an affordable alternative to the considerable expense of keeping a horse and buggy.

THE SUMMER RESORT HOTELS OF KITTERY
In the days before air-conditioning, trains and trolleys were a great benefit to the four large hotels in Kittery Point, allowing many middle-class families to leave behind the heat of Boston, New York and Philadelphia to spend several weeks at one of these truly wonderful hotels.

APPLEDORE HOUSE (1848-)
The first and oldest hotel in Kittery, as mentioned earlier, was the 1848 **Appledore House** on Appledore Island, Isles of Shoals, which lies ten miles out to sea but within the township of Kittery. Again Rosamond Thaxter recalls in her memoir, *Aunt Rozzie Remembers*:

> The Appledore Hotel was built by my great-grandfather, Thomas Laighton. Here the literary, artistic, and musical gathered from the 1850's to 1914, drawn by the life-giving air, the sailing and the fishing. Mostly, as moths to the flame, they gathered because of Celia Thaxter. She embodied the spirit of the place until her untimely death at only fifty-nine in 1894. The Appledore Hotel burned in 1914, and although no hotel replaced it, a new era began for Appledore when Dr. John Kingsbury built a Marine Biology Laboratory there.

HISTORY 📖

TRAINS, TROLLEYS & RESORT HOTELS

The Appledore House looks from photographs to be the largest of the Kittery/Isle of Shoals hotels. Comprised of three large buildings, each housing from 75 to 100 guests, it must have been truly grand. With each of the three buildings having a covered porch surrounding it, there was ample space for reading, strolling or sedate viewing of the ocean. Walks over the rough, treeless ground and scrambles on the rocks, fishing boat trips, swimming in a man-made ocean-water pool, breathing the brisk sea air, and, when it was out, basking in the glorious sunshine, were all activities for the hotel visitor.

Thomas Laighton and Levi Thaxter's Appledore House.

Built by Thomas Laighton and his friend Levi Thaxter, the Appledore House by the late 1800's became a mecca for writers and artists of the day, due primarily to Celia Thaxter, Levi's young wife and Thomas Laighton's daughter, who had grown up on the islands. An accomplished poet and essayist, Celia attracted the writer John Greenleaf Whittier and the artist Childe Hassam, among many others, to her "salon." (See page 28.)

A second Isles of Shoals hotel was built on Star Island in 1873 and after burning to the ground, was rebuilt the next year. This hotel, **The Oceanic**, survives today. Built by John Poor (of Stickney & Poor spice fame) the Oceanic was a success in its own right. By 1876, Oscar and Cedric Laighton had bought it, operating it in tandem with the Appledore House for several more years. By the turn of the century, the resort hotel era was coming to a close. Appledore House burned in 1914 and the Oceanic was later bought by the Star Island Corporation. Today this hotel, the only one still in existence, operates as a religious retreat (summer months only) for people of all ages. For more information, visit the Star Island website: www.starisland.org., and see also pages 28 and 29.

It is probable that the success of the Appledore House and the Oceanic gave rise to the four mainland hotels in Kittery Point.

PEPPERRELL HOTEL (1872-1923)
The **Pepperrell Hotel** was the oldest of the Kittery Point hotels. Built in 1872, it was situated opposite Frisbee's Store atop a sizeable hill.

From its lofty vantage point, the Pepperrell Hotel commanded a fine view of the harbor. Built by Edward Stafford, it had 48 rooms and was the longest-lasting of the on-shore hotels. After 79 years in service, it was partially consumed by fire in 1923 and closed.

The Pepperrell Hotel.

POCAHONTAS HOTEL (1885-1904)

The **Pocahontas Hotel** was the next to be built, located at the end of Gerrish Island right at the entrance to the harbor. A handsome, spacious 4-story building with a single central tower, it was built in 1885 by Samuel Jennison.

The 1885 Pocahontas Hotel.

The Pocahontas Hotel's 77 rooms and 7 guest cottages could accommodate 200 guests. Visitors could take a variety of long walks in the woods as well as along the beach at low tide. Horse and buggy excursions were offered to the top of Mount Agamenticus in York. One can easily see the attraction of both the train and especially the delightful trolley car rides for all of these summer visitors.

The Pocahontas Hotel was torn down in 1904 to make way for the construction of **Fort Foster**. From 1904 through World War I and World War II, the fort was home to, first, the US Coast Artillery Corp and then to the US Army. It is now a public park owned by the town of Kittery (see page 47).

PARKFIELD HOTEL (1887-1935)

The **Parkfield Hotel**, built two years later just south of the Frisbee Store, was run by Jessee Frisbee. A smaller hotel of only 35 rooms, it faced the water on Pepperrell Cove. Its large veranda's classic rocking chairs provided a great spot to view the harbor and Whaleback Light. This popular hotel burned down in 1935.

The Parkfield Hotel.

CHAMPERNOWNE HOTEL (1890-1923)

The last resort hotel built in Victorian Kittery Point was the **Champernowne Hotel**, at the end of Lawrence Lane. Opened in 1890 by Horace Mitchell, it had 98 rooms and 34 baths. This handsome 4-story, 2-towered hotel was encircled by a covered porch where one could watch croquet being played on the lawn leading down to the harbor. Mitchell, a leading figure and politician in Kittery, who also served as postmaster, lived in Sparhawk Hall across the street from Lawrence Lane. Sparhawk Hall, said to have

The Champernowne Hotel.

been the most beautiful example of colonial architecture in New England, unfortunately no longer exists. During World War I, the Champernowne Hotel housed navy yard workers. It was eventually torn down in 1923.

ROCK REST (ca. 1930-1974)

Wealthy families continued to summer in elaborate "cottages" along the coast of southern Maine, long after the last resort hotel closed. Their staffs of primarily African-American cooks, maids and chauffeurs developed the same fondness for the area as their employers did, often returning through the years as guests themselves at area lodgings that welcomed black guests. Only one, **Rock Rest,** known far and wide to African-American travelers as "the" place to stay in Kittery, still survives and will soon enjoy a much-needed restoration. Read more about this unique survivor on page 76.

THE END OF AN ERA

The availability and affordability of the automobile, along with improved roads and highways, brought an end to the electric trolleys and with them, the resort hotels. It is sad that none of these hotels or the trolley survives today, but with postcards and slides, we keep their memories alive.

Sources:
John D. Bardwell, **The Diary of the Portsmouth, Kittery and York Electric Railroad**. Portsmouth, NH: 1986, Peter E. Randall, Publisher.
O. R. Cummings, **York County Trolleys**.
Stephen Estes, *Remarks on Kittery Point's Resort Hotels.*
Rosmond Thaxter, **Aunt Rozzie Remembers**. Kittery Historical and Naval Museum, 1996.

Websites:
www.SeacoastNH.com

THE STORY OF THE
RICE PUBLIC LIBRARY

One of the tallest permanent structures in the town of Kittery is the **Rice Public Library.** In 1858, Arabella Rice, of Portsmouth, NH, left a bequest of $30,000 to create the Rice Free Public Library, in memory of her father, Robert Rice, a seaman who hailed from Kittery. The bequest to Kittery, "for educational purposes," inaugurated a literary legacy that has lasted more than a century.

The 1888 Rice Public Library.

In 1874 the Trustees, with old local names like Safford, Spinney, Wentworth and Wilson, opened a room in the Austin Block of Wallingford Square to house about a thousand volumes.

In 1888, the single room on the Square was replaced by the Victorian-era Queen Anne style Rice building, a block away from the library's original site. The structure on Wentworth Street, designed by S.S. Woodcock of Boston, was constructed of Philadelphia brick, and was embellished with marble steps, granite sills and a fine oak interior. The total cost for the building and furnishings was

$18,500. Today the building is listed on the National Registry of Historic Places.

By 1900, a librarian was hired to change the catalogue to the Dewey Decimal System; the library's titles, authors and subject headings were all duly entered by hand in "catalogue script." The cataloguing included numerous volumes of *The Harvard Classics*, a relic of earlier years. This last was a blessing, as by the mid-1960s, this collection was the only source in the library for classical writings.

By 1903, the library consisted of six thousand volumes. At that time there were both a Ladies' Reading Room and a Gentlemen's Reading Room. The curved counter in the main room on the first floor once had a gate connecting the two halves, to remind patrons that they were not allowed in the stacks. Obviously, it was all right for the librarian to climb the ladders in her long skirts, but not for lady patrons to do so. Beside the literature, history, reference and genealogy collections, stuffed birds and remnants of uniforms and flags decorated the interior. The library was also used as a meeting place for veterans of the Civil War's Grand Army of the Republic. The scrolled iron balcony over the main entrance served as an ideal spot for viewing passing parades.

By the mid-twentieth century, Arabella's lovely Queen Anne library was rapidly becoming a shabby old lady. The Gentlemen's Reading Room had become a reference room full of out-of-date encyclopedias and other ephemera; across the hall, the Ladies' Reading Room housed children's literature. The collection in the main room was aging, out-dated and limited. The only Hemingway title was the reasonably safe *The Snows of Kilimanjaro*. Faulkner was represented only by *The Reivers*. On the other hand, there were shelves of poorly mended and infrequently borrowed Grace Livingstonhill and Emily Loring novels. Both sides of the library grounds were used as a parking lot for shipyard workers.

In 1964-65, a series of changes began that finally brought the Rice Lbrary into the twentieth century. The first floor children's room was obviously inadequate and there was no more room available. The second floor, housing the stuffed bird collection, Civil War memorabilia and other antiquities, was summarily stripped,

its content of books dumped into a basement room with a dirt floor and extremely basic lighting. The second floor room was transformed into a "brown box," its plastered walls covered with matching brown paneling. The beautiful ceiling was covered with suspended tiles, the floor with lighter brown tiles. The first floor's inadequate shelving was carried upstairs, along with whatever else could be taken from the building. A large table was donated by a board member; folding chairs were added here and there... and that was it. The fire escape was also added at this time, an absolute necessity before the room could be reopened. When the collection had been weeded and the books moved, the then librarian celebrated by purchasing new encyclopedias, replacing the former 1934-35 editions.

The second floor "brown box," revitalized.

In 1989, with the addition of the Taylor building, the subsequent division of the collection between the two structures relieved a long-standing space problem. Situated diagonally across Wentworth Road from the Rice building, the Taylor building was the former Southern York County District Court House.

Named in a vote by Kittery school children for the prominent town physician and one-time library trustee, Paul Taylor. The annex was redesigned and renovated and now houses the children's collection, audio/visual material (cassettes, videos, CDs, DVDs and books on tape), mysteries and both adult and children's general fiction, plus recent periodicals. It is also the location of the Friends of the Rice Library's on-going book sale, which helps support some of the library's numerous programs.

Coincident with the acquisition of the Taylor building, the Library received a bequest from Almyra Roberts, a long-time patron, which funded work in the Taylor building. The first floor was reinforced with steel beams to accommodate the weight of books and opened up into stack areas and a reading ell. An administration desk was created utilizing the former judges' bench. The basement was partitioned to house the children's book collection and the children's program. The transfer of books from the Rice building to Taylor was performed by a human chain of Kittery citizens on a Saturday, under the direction of the Rotary Club; the Kittery police blocked off Wentworth Street while the task was accomplished.

Once the move was completed, the entire Rice building was cleaned, the brick work repointed, the slate roof repaired and new storm windows added. New lighting was installed throughout, with painting and varnishing done where needed. The former children's room was completely remodeled; the removal of the false ceiling on the second floor revealed the original vaulted ceiling created by the builder. Hand-blown glass panels were preserved and cleaned and the woodwork stabilized. To house a growing collection, a new mezzanine, occupying the periphery of the room, was added, accessed by a grand double stairway.

Change happily continued. The Harborside Garden Club, with the urging of trustee Elizabeth Brewster, landscaped and planted the left parking lot along one side of the building. About six years after the Rice renovation, another donation enabled an upgrade of the Howells room in Rice's basement. Tastefully engineered stacks were added, and under-floor heating, carpeting and new lighting were installed, preserving sufficient space for a medium-size meeting room.

By 2005, the two buildings contained over 56,000 titles, along with copying machines, computers, staff offices, the Kay Howells Meeting Room, inter-library loan services, and multiple programs for adults and children, including reading and discussion groups, poetry and writing workshops, and a recently added monthly film festival. The current staff of eight has begun transferring the computerized catalogue to the Maine state MINERVA system, enabling Rice's patrons to access a multitude of resources.

Coordinating with the adjacent towns, the Rice Public Library serves a local community of over 9,500. Major operational funding is provided by the Town of Kittery. Institutional administration is overseen by a seven-member public Board of Trustees, while daily management of the facility and specialized staff is the bailiwick of a professional library director. Additional funding comes from the Friends of the Rice Library, which publishes a quarterly newsletter, as well as from grants and donations from area businesses and individuals.

However, unless you actually come inside the Rice building, you cannot experience the magic of this special library. We welcome you all.

The Rice Public Library, 8 Wentworth Street, Kittery, ME 03904 207-439-1553; www.rice.lib.me.us.

THINGS TO DO TODAY

WHAT TO DO IN KITTERY

Kittery offers many varied activities both indoors and out. The following is a sampling of the town's major attractions. Consult the 2-page map at the front of the guide or the maps in the Driving Tour (pages 58-61) to help interpret the directions for the activities below. When you are in Kittery, you do not need to dial the area code (207), but you do if calling from Portsmouth, NH (whose own area code is 603), and, of course, from outside the area.

OUTDOOR ACTIVITIES

DRIVING TOUR
Take the Driving Tour (page 62) to acquaint yourself with the area. The tour runs basically from Badger's Island along Route 103 to Brave Boat Harbor at the Kittery/York town line.

Fort Foster beach head.

WALKING 👣
Fort Foster

Directions: Drive north on Route 103 and turn RIGHT onto Gerrish Island Lane. Continue on, crossing Chauncey Creek Road and immediately onto the Gerrish Island Bridge. Turn RIGHT at the "T" onto Pocahontas Road. Drive for one mile until you come to the gate of Fort Foster.

>>Fort Foster, owned by the Town of Kittery, is open year round, but driving and parking inside the gate are available only from Memorial Day to Labor Day. (Parking year-round is permitted outside the gate on Pocahontas Road.) The park is open seven days a week from 10 AM to 8 PM. A day pass for a car and its occupants is $10.00. Walk-in or Bike-in passes are $5.00 and children under twelve years are admitted for $1.00. There are trails along the shore and in the interior of the park. Restrooms are available during the May to Sept. season. At low tide, walking on the hard sand beaches is excellent and scrambling on the rocks can be fun.

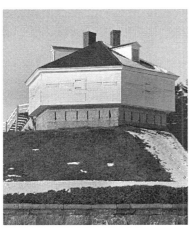

Fort McClary.

Fort McClary

Directions: Drive north on Route 103. Less than a ½ mile after crossing the Spruce Creek bridge, the park will be on the RIGHT.

>>There are no trails at Fort McClaryv, but rather an open area near the shore to wander. Fort McClary is open year-round from dawn to dusk. A modest voluntary fee is suggested. A restroom is available during late spring to late fall. For some of the history of Fort McClary, and information about playground and picnic facilities, see page 70.

Kittery Town Forest

Directions: Drive ½ mile from US Route 1 going east on Haley Road or, coming from Route 103 (Pepperrell Road), drive 2½ miles going to the west on Haley Road. The Forest is on the north side of Haley Road. The sign, though large, is difficult to see from the road. Parking is limited.

>>The Forest consists of 72 acre area, has 2 hiking trails and is open throughout the year. There are no restroom facilities nor is there a fee for admittance. There is a caution about walking in the

Forest: hunting is also allowed year-round except on Sundays. Do stay on the trails if you decide to walk there.

Rogers Park
Directions: Drive on Rogers Road (Route 236) east (or west) and turn LEFT (or RIGHT) on Dion Avenue. Follow Dion Avenue until it curves to the LEFT and dead ends. Park in the cul-de-sac.
>>Several trails run along the wooded shore of Spruce Creek and into the interior. There are no restrooms and no fee.

Seapoint and Crescent Beaches
Directions: Traveling north on Route 103, turn RIGHT on Cutts Island Lane and cross the causeway onto the island. The Rachel Carson Preserve will be on your LEFT. Continue on less than a mile to a small parking lot on the RIGHT. This is the only place for non-residents to park. Walk on the road which curves into the beach (about 500 feet beyond the parking lot).
>>The Town of Kittery owns and oversees the Seapoint and Crescent sand beaches. The point separating them was given to the Kittery Land Trust by Rosamund Thaxter. The area is open year round. You are welcome to walk the point and beaches, being mindful of some regulations. There is no camping. Fires are by permit only (issued at Town Hall) and NO consumption of alcohol is allowed. Dogs are permitted on the beaches but must be on leash. Dogs are not allowed, however, from June 15th through Sept. 10th between the hours of 10 AM and 5 PM. Cleaning up after your animal is strictly enforced. No trash collection or restrooms are available.

Rachel Carson Preserve
Directions: See above for the directions to Seapoint Beach. A pull-out on Seapoint Road next to the Preserve can accommodate a few cars.
>>The Rachel Carson Preserve, part of a 10-parcel system of conserved properties extending from Kittery as far north as Cape Elizabeth, protects areas of marsh and a fresh-water wetland estuary totalling 4700 acres. Numerous trails provide access.

Kittery Land Trust
>>The preservation of Kittery's seashore, marsh, wetlands and woodlands is the work and goal of the Kittery Land Trust, a non-profit, volunteer-run organization that owns or holds easements

on nearly 300 acres of land. The Trust invites you to enjoy two of these properties: the headlands at Seapoint Beach, as mentioned on the prior page, and the Cooks Wetland. The latter is an open water marsh full of birds, ducks and a pair of nesting swans. (*Park at the public lot on the southeast corner of US Route 1 and Walker Street. Walk north on US Route1 to the Beach Pea Bakery, which will be on your left, and access the marsh from the rear of the bakery.*) For more information and events, go on line to www. kitterylandtrust.org.

Trails at the Rachel Carson Preserve pass through a wooded area that leads to the marshes at Brave Boat Harbor.

SWIMMING

Seapoint and Crescent Beaches
See directions and description, page 48.

Fort Foster
See directions, page 47.
>> Wonderful beaches are available at Fort Foster.

Kittery Town Pool
Directions: Drive around the Kittery traffic circle and exit on Old Post Road (the road between the US Route 1 Bypass and US Route 1). Travel south on Old Post until you come to the Memorial Field ball fields on the LEFT.

>>The Kittery Town Pool, an outdoor pool operated by the Recreation Department for recreational swimming and lessons, is open from June through Labor Day. "Swim and Movies" is a weekly evening event from late June to mid-August. It's lots of fun watching movies while floating around! Popcorn is even served. The fees for swimming, lessons and events are modest. Call the Recreation Dept. at 207-439-3800 for further information.

PICNICKING
Fort Foster

Directions: See directions page 47.

>>There are picnic grounds looking out to the harbor entrance and the sea, and grills and fire-pits are available. NO alcohol consumption is allowed. Dogs must be on a leash at all times and you must clean up after your pets. The park entrance fee includes use of the picnic grounds.

Fort McClary Picnic and Play Ground

Directions: See directions for Fort McClary (page 47) and look to the north side of Route 103 for the picnic and playgrounds. Parking is available inside the grounds late spring through fall.

>>You will find several picnic sites and grills in the park as well as playground equipment. Dogs must be on a leash at all times, and you need to clean up after your pet. A modest voluntary fee is suggested.

Rogers Park
Directions: See directions page 48.
>>There are no tables here, but there are a few benches and a nice shoreline for viewing Spruce Creek while picnicking. Dog rules apply here, of course.

BOATING
Public Boat Launching Ramps
>>There are two public boat launching ramps in the town. Traip Academy boat ramp is off of Williams Avenue by the high school. Drive to the far side of the school parking lot and you will see the ramp to the LEFT. The Town Dock at Pepperrell Cove in Kittery Point, across from the Kittery Point Post Office, also has a boat launching area.

Kayaking and Canoeing
>>Kittery Trading Post, on US Route 1 in the Outlet Mall area, offers kayak and canoe lessons in local waters beginning in April and running through October. KTP sells, but does NOT rent, the boats. Throughout the year, KTP gives weekly seminars and classes on outdoor skills and topics. For information call 888-587-6246 or check their website, www.kitterytradingpost.com, for the schedule of the seminars and events.

Captain and Patty's
>>Captain Neil Odams runs a tour of the Piscataqua River basin emphasizing the history of the area. Aboard the **SIR WILLIAM PEPPERRELL,** there are opportunities to see and photograph lighthouses and harbor sites. Tours begin at Pepperrell Cove at the Town Dock, from June 1st to October 15th Tuesday through Sunday, 9 AM to 6 PM. Reservations for the 6 PM tour are necessary. All tours last for more than an hour. Call 207-439-8976 for more information.

Saboutime Sailing
>>Captain John Harkless runs the only sailing tour in the harbor. These are real sailing excursions with very little use of the engine. The tours are out of Pepperrell Cove and are arranged by calling 207-439-6248. Sailing cruises, on an Islander 37, last about 3 hours from 9 AM to 12 noon and from 2 PM to 5 PM, seven days a week. Evening cruises from 7 to 9 PM may also be booked. All-day and longer charters are available. The sailing season starts in May and

lasts into October. You are welcome to bring your own food and drink or Saboutime will provide a catered meal. Sailing lessons on a J/24 are also an option. See the website, www.saboutimesailing. com for more information.

Seafari Charters
>>This charter company runs fishing, scuba, whale watching and harbor tours from 9 Island Avenue on Badger's Island. The season runs from April through October. Call 207-439-5068 for more information and reservations.

Portsmouth Harbor Cruises
>>The **HERITAGE** tours the harbor, Isles of Shoals and inland Piscataqua River out of Portsmouth, N.H. Call 800-776-0915 or see the website, www.portsmouthharbor.com.

Isles of Shoals Steamship Company
>>The large double-decker tourist ship you see plying the Piscataqua is the **M/V THOMAS LAIGHTON**. Cruises take sightseers on explorations of Portsmouth Harbor, Great Bay and around the Isles of Shoals. Dinner, lighthouse and party cruises are also available out of Portsmouth, N.H. Call 800-441-4620 or go on line to the website, www.islesofshoals.com.

Island Cruises
>>This tour company out of Rye Harbor in Rye, NH, t runs excursions out to the Isles of Shoals from late May through September. Call Captain Sue Reynolds, of the **UNCLE OSCAR**, for more information at 603-964-6446 or visit the website, www.uncleoscar.com.

FISHING
>>Fishing licenses are not required for salt water fishing. You may try your luck at the Town Wharf off of Government Street near Wallingford Square. As you travel northeast on Government St. turn RIGHT at the Corner Pub and then sharply RIGHT down to the wharf. Parking is very limited here. It is suggested that you park in the public lot by Rice Library.

The Spruce Creek Bridge on Route 103 is a favorite of fisherman, as is the long pier at Fort Foster. Surf fishing is allowed at Seapoint and Crescent beaches.

Pier at Fort Foster

OTHER OUTDOOR RECREATION

Ballparks
>>There are four ball parks in the area. Memorial Field on Old Post Road and Emery Field at the Recreation Center on Cole Ave. are under Recreation Department auspices. You are welcome to use the field in front of Frisbee School on Rogers Road or the fields and track at Shapleigh Middle School at the crossroads of Stevenson and Manson in north Kittery off of Route 236.

Coastline Golf & Sport
>>An entertainment center with mini-golf, indoor golf, batting cages, driving range and more. Located at 506 US Route 1, Kittery, ME. 03904, 207-439-7529. Go to their website for more info:www. coastlinegolfandsport.com.

Running the Dog
>>You may exercise your pet at Fort Foster, Fort McClary, Rogers Park, Kittery Town Farm Forest, Seapoint and Crescent beaches. ALL of these areas have leash laws, so consult the posted rules at each entrance. You are required to clean up after your pet.

Festivals and Concerts
The Recreation Department organizes a Water Festival in July and a Winter Festival in January. In addition, Summer Concerts with a variety of music are held at Memorial Field (Old Post Road) from July through August. The concerts are held on Wednesday evenings and are free. Call the Rec. Dept. at 207-439-3800 for information or go on line at www.kittery.org.

Cross Country Skiing and Snowshoeing
Fort Foster, Kittery Town Forest, Rogers Park and Rachel Carson Preserve are all suitable for cross country skiing and snowshoeing when there is plenty of snow. You can ice skate on the pond at Fort McClary when there is ice.

INDOOR ACTIVITIES

MUSEUM

Kittery Historical and Naval Museum
Directions: Drive around the Kittery traffic circle and take US Route 1 going north. Immediately at the junction of US Route 1 and Rogers Road, you will see the Museum on the RIGHT, next to the Kittery Town Hall.

This museum is a virtual treasure trove of the old and cherished artifacts of Kittery. Exhibits tell of everyday people: seafarers, fishermen, merchants, craftsmen, farmers, homemakers, artists and children. It also has many naval antiquities. The Kittery Historical & Naval Museum is open June to Columbus Day, Tuesday through Saturday from 10 AM to 4 PM, or by appointment. The Museum has gift items and books about the area. The admission fee is modest. Call 207-439-3080 for additional information.

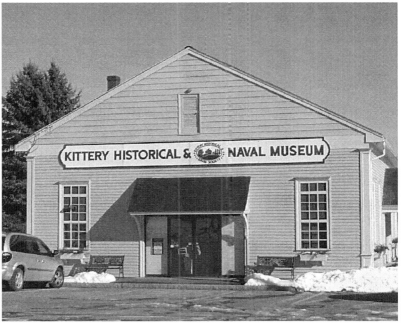

The Kittery Historical and Naval Museum.

GALLERIES AND THE ART SCENE

Kittery Art Association

Directions: 8 Coleman Avenue is off Route 103 in Kittery Point, just south of Cap'n Simeon's Restaurant. The Art Association is open Thursdays from 3 to 6 PM, Saturday 12 noon to 6 PM and on Sundays, 12 noon to 5 PM.

>>The Kittery Art Association is a non-profit organization that was founded in 1958. Since a January 1999 fire, the gallery has been restored and exists in what was once a fire station for Kittery Point. Its mission is

to promote knowledge and stimulate interest in and appreciation of the creative arts in the community. It does this by holding exhibits, by providing instruction to encourage art interest in our youth and all ages and by enriching the arts in our community.

Art exhibits are on display year-round and the Music Series holds events, usually one Friday evening per month January through June. Art and Music classes and public events are offered to the community. You can check the web site for more information, www.kitteryartassociation.org, or e-mail: information@kittery-artassociation.org. The mailing address is P. O. Box 44, Kittery Point, ME 03905.

Haley Farm Gallery
Direction: The Gallery is located at 178 Haley Road, off US Route 1, north of the Kittery Outlet Malls. Look for Yummies Candy at the corner of US Route 1 and Haley Road. Turn RIGHT on Haley Road and continue for less than a mile. The Gallery is housed in the yellow barn, once part of a large dairy operation. Parking is available behind the barn, off Hutchins Cove Road.
>>Haley Farm Gallery features all types of art media and has a gift shop as well, with art gifts from around the world. The Gallery is open March through December, Wednesday through Saturday from 11 AM to 5 P.M. For further information, call 207-439-2669 or check the website, www.haleygallery.com.

Just Us Chickens
Directions: 29 Government Street is in Kittery Foreside, just west of Wallingford Square. Parking is available in the rear.
>>The co-op features painting, weaving, ceramics, jewelry and a variety of unique fine arts and crafts by local artists. It is open year round, Tuesday through Saturday from 10 AM to 5 P.M. Call 207-439-4209 for information or go on line at www.justuschickens.net.

Other Studios
>>While you are in the Kittery Foreside area check out Gail Sauter's studio at 9 Government Street. The studio may be open by chance or call for an appointment at 207-439-0223. Gail works in oils and pastels and paints primarily local scenes specializing in waterscapes. Mary Margaret Sweeney is a printmaker of etchings at 39 Government Street. She is open by appointment only by calling 207-439-9447.

OTHER IDEAS

Recreation Department
>>Year round programs for toddlers through senior citizens are sponsored by the Rec. Dept. Crafts, dance, sports, trips, adventures and after school programs are examples of the offerings. Call 207-439-3800 for information or go on line at www.kittery.org.

State of Maine Tourism Association
>>The Maine Tourist Bureau, located north of the Outlet Malls between US Route 1 and Interstate 95, can be entered from either of the parallel roads. It has an abundance of materials about touring the area and points of interest in Maine.

A familiar sight along the tidal waterways of Maine.

DRIVING TOUR

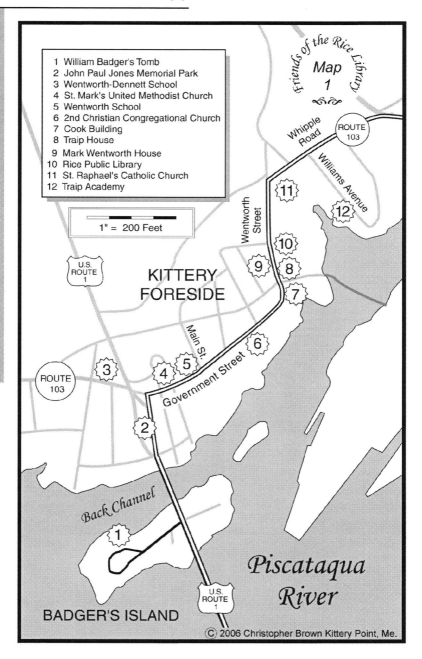

1 William Badger's Tomb
2 John Paul Jones Memorial Park
3 Wentworth-Dennett School
4 St. Mark's United Methodist Church
5 Wentworth School
6 2nd Christian Congregational Church
7 Cook Building
8 Traip House
9 Mark Wentworth House
10 Rice Public Library
11 St. Raphael's Catholic Church
12 Traip Academy

Friends of the Rice Library

Map 1

1" = 200 Feet

ROUTE 103

Whipple Road

Williams Avenue

U.S. ROUTE 1

KITTERY FORESIDE

Wentworth Street

Main St.

Government Street

ROUTE 103

Back Channel

Piscataqua River

BADGER'S ISLAND

U.S. ROUTE 1

© 2006 Christopher Brown Kittery Point, Me.

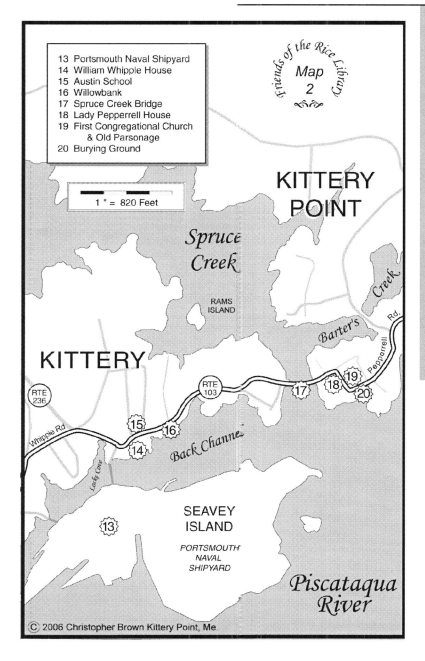

13 Portsmouth Naval Shipyard
14 William Whipple House
15 Austin School
16 Willowbank
17 Spruce Creek Bridge
18 Lady Pepperrell House
19 First Congregational Church
      & Old Parsonage
20 Burying Ground

Friends of the Rice Library
Map
2

1 " = 820 Feet

KITTERY
POINT

Spruce
Creek

RAMS
ISLAND

Barter's

Creek

KITTERY

Pepperrell Rd.

RTE
236

RTE
103

17

18 19

20

Whipple Rd

15

16

Back Channel

Lock Cove

14

SEAVEY
ISLAND

PORTSMOUTH
NAVAL
SHIPYARD

13

Piscataqua
River

© 2006 Christopher Brown Kittery Point, Me.

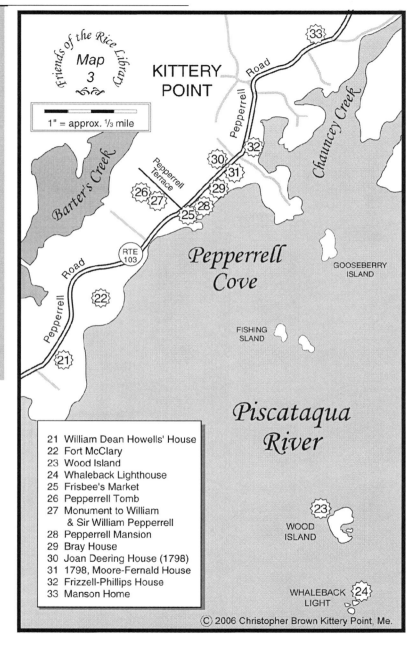

KITTERY POINT

Friends of the Rice Library
Map
3

1" = approx. ⅓ mile

Road

33

Pepperrell

Chauncey Creek

Pepperrell Terrace

32

30
31
29
28

26 27

25

Barter's Creek

RTE 103

22

Pepperrell Road

21

Pepperrell Cove

GOOSEBERRY ISLAND

FISHING SLAND

Piscataqua River

WOOD ISLAND

23

WHALEBACK LIGHT

24

21 William Dean Howells' House
22 Fort McClary
23 Wood Island
24 Whaleback Lighthouse
25 Frisbee's Market
26 Pepperrell Tomb
27 Monument to William
     & Sir William Pepperrell
28 Pepperrell Mansion
29 Bray House
30 Joan Deering House (1798)
31 1798, Moore-Fernald House
32 Frizzell-Phillips House
33 Manson Home

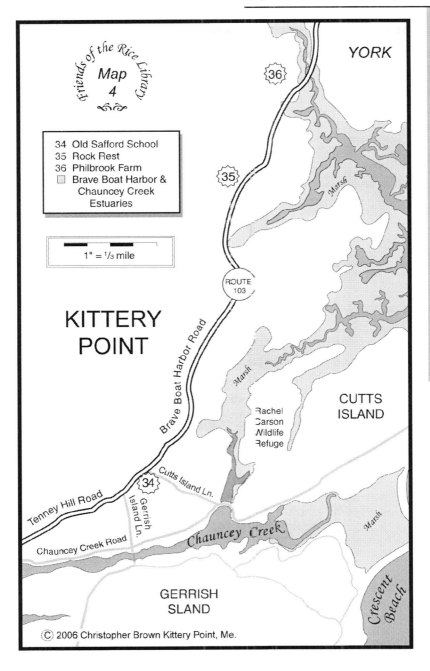

Friends of the Rice Library

Map
4

YORK

36

34 Old Safford School
35 Rock Rest
36 Philbrook Farm
☐ Brave Boat Harbor &
Chauncey Creek
Estuaries

35

Marsh

1" = ⅓ mile

ROUTE
103

KITTERY
POINT

Brave Boat Harbor Road

Marsh

CUTTS
ISLAND

Rachel
Carson
Wildlife
Refuge

Cutts Island Ln.

34

Gerrish Island Ln.

Tenney Hill Road

Chauncey Creek Road

Chauncey Creek

Marsh

GERRISH
ISLAND

Crescent Beach

Ⓒ 2006 Christopher Brown Kittery Point, Me.

KITTERY DRIVING TOUR
OF ROUTE 103

You will find many lovely homes, interesting buildings and monuments along the roads of Kittery. The following suggested driving tour identifies some of these historic sites in our town. The homes and buildings are privately owned so there are no tours of them, but hopefully this guide will encourage and satisfy your curiosity. The tour route covers about 6 miles and will take about 30 minutes to drive without any stops. When you do stop on Route 103, be cautious of where you park, particularly when getting out of your car. During the summer months there are many bicycles and the road is narrow and quite busy.

Three bridges cross the swift-flowing Piscataqua River between Portsmouth, NH, and Kittery. This tour starts after crossing on the southernmost bridge, **Memorial Bridge** or **US Route 1**. This tour brings you into Kittery by way of **Badger's Island**. (The coast of Maine is chock-full of islands and often you are unaware of traveling from the mainland onto these islands.)

As you travel north, turn LEFT on Badger Island West Road. Continue a short distance; take the RIGHT side of the fork and park on the side of the road near the tall yellow condo building. Walk up the granite steps to the hill to **(1) Badger's Tomb** and the cemetery. This island was the site of shipbuilding by William Badger in the

1700s. Badger built and launched the **USS RANGER**, a famous American ship, for John Paul Jones in 1777. The shipwright's tomb is worth a side visit to view its lovely setting, its touching inscription and the small cemetery itself. (See also page 3.)

(There are many family cemeteries in Kittery; you need to ask permission of the land owners to walk among the gravestones. Some of these old cemeteries are on public land, such as **Badger's Tomb** and the **Burying Ground**, later on the tour, where one may respectfully view the stones.)

(2) Detail from "Sacrifices of War," the powerful memorial to those fallen in the First World War.

Drive around the loop, retrace your steps back to US Route 1 and turn LEFT. As you travel over the bridge and onto the mainland, you will see directly ahead of you the **(2) John Paul Jones Memorial Park**. Find a parking spot as best you can. A walk through this entrance to Kittery is worthwhile.

The centerpiece of this two-acre park is the granite and bronze **Monument to Sailors and Soldiers** by Basha Paeff completed in 1926. Two smaller monuments are also on view, one honoring the **Marines** and the other the **USS RANGER**.

DRIVING TOUR 🚕

Continue on down the one-way street you are on until it dead-ends at Government Street and look over to your LEFT, up the hill, at the 3-story brick building on the northwest corner of Government Street and US Route 1. This is the old **(3) Wentworth-Dennett School** which today houses artists' studios. Note the oversized and unique sculptures on the grounds. Well worth a stop if you have time and the inclination. The beautiful landscaping at the corner is the handiwork of Judie Kehl of Harbor Realtors, whose office is in the Stover House across the street.

(3) A giant armchair awaits the observant passerby.

Now turn RIGHT onto Government Street into what is known as the **Kittery Foreside**, the old downtown Kittery. You will see (4) **St. Mark's United Methodist Church** on the LEFT. A few doors further down on the LEFT, at 52 Government Street, is a tall brick two story building with the date 1868 predominantly displayed, originally the **(5) Wentworth School**, then the **Town Hall** and now a private home. Further down Government Street is the **(6) Second Christian Congregational Church,** on the RIGHT.

At the bend of Government Street, you will see before you the large, four-story gray building known as the **(7) Cook Building.** You are now in **Wallingford Square**, an historic, and once again, the bustling commercial center of Kittery.

(7) The Cook Building.

64 KITTERY & KITTERY POINT GUIDEBOOK

At the intersection of Government Street and Route 103 (specifically, 2 and 4 Wentworth Street) you will see a two and a half story Greek Revival style, cream-colored home on the RIGHT, the **(8) Traip House**, which stands near an entrance to the **Portsmouth Naval Shipyard** (note: the Shipyard is closed to the public).

Robert Traip, the successful businessman who built this lovely home, willed part of his estate to be used to establish a high school in Kittery. In 1905, his dream came true and **Traip Academy** opened. Traip's original name was Tripe which he changed for business reasons. The large cork elm standing in front of the Traip House is a state-acknowledged "Champion" and holds a proud spot on the Maine Register of Big Trees. A small plaque to the left of the tree gives more details.

The **(9) Mark Wentworth House**, at 9 Wentworth Street on the LEFT, was the home of General and Doctor Wentworth (both one in the

(8) The Traip House, and its "Champion" cork elm.

same fellow). Wentworth, commander of the 27th Maine regiment during the Civil War, was highly regarded as a doctor and citizen as well. The house is painted a bright yellow, with green shutters. The General's grave can be found in the alley to the RIGHT of the "We Care" dry cleaners in a small, well-tended cemetery.

The handsome **(10) Rice Public Library** building on the RIGHT is a fine example of the Romanesque Revival style, much in vogue at the end of the 19th century. See the section about the history and the current collections of the library on page **41**.

At this point Route 103 changes its name, becoming Whipple Road, and turns to the RIGHT at **(11) St. Raphael's** Catholic Church on the corner. **(12) Traip Academy** is down on Williams Avenue to the RIGHT. Continue on Whipple Road (still Route 103) to the intersection of Shapleigh Road (Route 236) and turn RIGHT.

The second entrance to the **(13) Portsmouth Naval Shipyard (see pages 9-22)** is located on Locke Cove. Also on Locke Cove is the

(13) Locals refer to he second entrance to the Portsmouth Naval Shipyard as the "back gate."

(14) The William Whipple House.

(14) William Whipple House (88 Whipple Road, set back on the RIGHT). Little of the original architectural style of the gray wooden home, built in 1665 as a garrison against Indian raids, remains. William Whipple, a signer of the Declaration of Independence, was born in this house.

As you continue, the two-story bright red **(15) Austin School,** with its distinctive bell tower, will catch your eye on the LEFT. Built in 1895 and named for the Reverend Daniel Austin, who lived in the neighborhood and gave the bell to the school, it is a private residence today, but you can see the school bell at the **Kittery Historical and Naval Museum** just off of US Route 1.

(15) A period photo of the old Austin School.

In a short while you will come to **(16)** **Willowbank** (124 Whipple Road), a large white home with black shutters on the RIGHT, overlooking the water. The estate, built in 1735, has been home to many local notables. The famous American painter, **John P. Benson**, owned the property and had a studio just across the street in the 1930s and 1940s. The waterway that 103 follows in this area is part of the Piscataqua River. It was once known as Crooked Lane. Today, the locals just call it the Back Channel.

In about a half a mile, you will drive across **(17)** the **Spruce Creek Bridge.** Look back to your LEFT and you will see the remains of the railroad/trolley trestle on the far shore, decaying and in disrepair, easily distinguished from current docks along the shore. Crossing the bridge, you have now entered **Kittery Point.**

(17) Spruce Creek Bridge welcomes you to Kittery Point.

Although you are still on Route 103, the road changes names three times before reaching the **York** town line. At the bridge it is known as **Pepperrell Road**; in less than 2 miles, its name changes to **Tenney Hill Road**; lastly, Route 103 becomes **Brave Boat Harbor Road.**

There are many lovely structures along the way and this tour will point out just a few. You can always go to the **Kittery Historical and Naval Museum** just off US Route 1 next to Town Hall for further information about places not covered in this tour.

Just past Spruce Creek Bridge and after the curve in the road on your RIGHT stands one of the more imposing homes in Kittery Point. The **(18) Lady Pepperrell House**, built in 1760 for the widow of **Sir William Pepperrell**, is a designated historic home. The cream colored building is in the Georgian style. For more details, see pages 4-5.

(18) The Lady Pepperrell House.

(19) The First Congregational Church and Parsonage.

Across the road stands the **(19) First Congregational Church** and **Parsonage**. The church was built in 1730 as the First Parish Meeting House. Its cupola replaced a traditional spire after several lightning strikes in the late 1800s.

The oldest section of the large white building on the property was built in 1729 as a parsonage for the first pastor, the Reverend John Newmarch, who served the church for 50 years. The parsonage, today a parish hall and community center, has recently been renovated and enlarged.

Across from the church on your RIGHT looking out to the river is the **(20) Burying Ground** which has served the community from the 1600s to present times. **Levi Thaxter**, the husband of the poet **Celia Thaxter**, is buried here. Levi was a scholar of the works of Robert Browning. Browning wrote the epitaph especially for the Thaxter gravestone which is on the left side by the water.

(20) The Burying Ground.

A few houses further up the road on the RIGHT is the **(21) William Dean Howells House** (36 Pepperrell Road), built in 1870 with a distinctive Mansard style roof. The wooden exterior is painted gray. The summer residence of Howells, author and editor of the *Atlantic Monthly*, it was visited by such notables as Mark Twain (Samuel Clemens), Nathaniel Hawthorne and Celia Thaxter. The complex is now owned by Harvard University and used by faculty visiting the area.

Continuing on, the state monument of **(22) Fort McClary** is on the RIGHT with the **Fort McClary picnic area/playground** on the LEFT. (see page **47**) Built in 1715 to protect Kittery against attack by sea, it was originally named Fort William in honor of William Pepperrell. The Pepperrells were Loyalists whose properties were confiscated following the Revolution, after which the fort was renamed in honor of Andrew McClary, a Revolutionary War soldier who died at Bunker Hill. The compound has undergone changes and additions over the years. Be sure to wander around the buildings

(22) Fort McClary.

and grounds which are maintained by the state of Maine. A small donation is requested. Restrooms are available spring through fall at both the fort and the picnic grounds.

As you look out to the ocean, you will see a long pier on the horizon on the LEFT side of the harbor entrance. That pier is at **Fort Foster** on Gerrish Island. Out from the pier is **(23) Wood Island,** with the remains of a Coast Guard life saving station.

(23) A ship makes its way into Portsmouth Harbor, past the old Coast Guard station to the left, and (24) Whaleback Light, to the right.

The Wood Island Coast Guard Station was used in the early 1900s as a base for rescuing ships and survivors at sea. The island structure is abandoned and approachable only by boat, an adventure NOT recommended. Next to Wood Island is **(24) Whaleback Light,** a stone lighthouse constructed in 1872, which marks the Kittery side of the harbor entrance. This is such a nice view. The river marks the Maine-New Hampshire state line.

(25) Frisbee's Market, 178 years old and still going strong.

About a half a mile further on the RIGHT you will see **(25) Frisbee's Market**, established in 1828, the oldest family-owned market in the country. (See pages 81-82). Turn RIGHT into **Bellamy Lane**, just after the market, and drive on down to **Pepperrell Cove** onto the **Town Dock.**

The cove is a working harbor for the local fishermen. Their small boats and dinghies are docked on the left while pleasure boats are on the right of the main pier. It is enjoyable to just look out at the boats and watch the activities. Look back at the harbor side of the **Captain Simeon's Restaurant** and note the building. This was an earlier site of the **Frisbee Store**. The land once ended at the back of this structure with a wharf. After Frisbee's moved closer to the road, this building was used as a ships' outfitter or "chandlery."

Across from the market, find a parking spot and walk up the road on the LEFT side of the **(26) Kittery Point Post Office.** At the top of a small hill, surrounded by cedars, are the **(27) Pepperrell Tomb** and the **monument to William Pepperrell and Sir William Pepperrell.** Refer to the early history and forefathers, pages 4-5, for more information about these illustrious citizens.

(27) The Pepperrell Tomb.

Return to Route 103 and across the road you will see a dark, almost black, gambrel-roofed home. This is the **(28) Pepperrell Mansion,** next to Frisbee's Market, the home that **William Pepperrell** built in 1682 and the birthplace of his son, **Sir William.** The noted

(28) The Pepperrell Mansion.

nautical woodcarver, **John Haley Bellamy**, famous to this day for his carvings of eagles, stern boards and figureheads, lived in a small house on this property (see page 5). It is worth a visit to the **Kittery Historical and Naval Museum** to see three of Bellamy's eagles.

In 2005, a classic Bellamy eagle sold at auction for $666,000.

Just two doors on the RIGHT (100 Pepperrell Road) is a large rambling house known as the **(29) Bray House**, built in 1662 by John Bray, a shipwright. It is reported to be the oldest house in Maine and one of the oldest in the country.

Continuing along, you come to the **(30) Joan Deering House** (111 Pepperrell Road) on the LEFT, which was built as a tavern in 1700.

(31) The 1798 House.

Just beyond the Deering House on the RIGHT is **(31) a** red house (116 Pepperrell Road) marked with the date '**1798.**' Built by sea captain **John Moore**, the house was sold to **Peletiah Fernald** in 1800 and remained in the Fernald family until the late 1800s, when it became the residence of writer and artist George S. Wasson, about whose 1903 novel, *Cap'n Simeon's Store,* you will hear more later. Wasson learned to carve from his neighbor John Bellamy (see pages 5 and 74) and carved the '1798' sign that distinguishes the house to this day.

The **(32) Frizzell-Phillips House** (154 Pepperrell Road) on the RIGHT, was built in 1763 and was also used as a tavern at one point. Actually, there were several taverns in this neighborhood in the early days.

At 177 Pepperrell Road, on the LEFT, is the **(33) Manson House** which was built around 1675 on the Isles of Shoals. It was moved to the mainland about 1750. The original house was smaller and has been expanded through the years.

Continue on until you come to the forked intersection of Pepperrell Road and Chauncey Creek Road. At this point, Route 103 bears LEFT up the hill and becomes **Tenney Hill Road**.

About a half a mile further on, the old **(34) Safford School** stands

at the crossroads of Route 103 (now Brave Boat Harbor Road) and Cutt's Island Lane. Children attended this modest one-room elementary school, built in 1871, until the early 1940s.

As you drive to the next site, the marshes and sea can often be seen along the RIGHT side of the road. You can catch a glimpse of the old trolley trestle described on page 34 across the marshes.

(34) The old one-room Safford School.

Continuing on, you come to the old **(35) Rock Rest Guest House**, at 167 Brave Boat Harbor Road on your LEFT. This modest and much expanded New England cape is eligible for listing on the National Register of Historic Places and is about to undergo a well-deserved restoration.

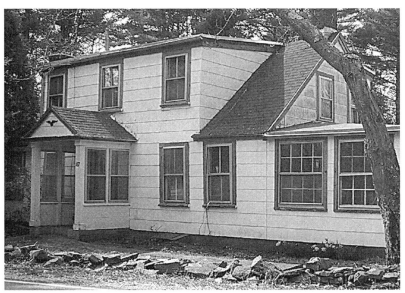

(35) One proposal under consideration for the future of Rock Rest: housing for visiting scholars in the area to study the Seacoast region's African-American history.

From the 1930s to 1974, a period when black travelers were still subject to discrimination in tourist accommodations, Hazel and Clayton Sinclair welcomed their fellow African-Americans to vacation with them in Maine. With two guest rooms in the main house, and an additional five above the garage, Rock Rest could accommodate up to sixteen guests, many of whom returned year after year.

In the 1950s, one of the Sinclairs' double rooms could be enjoyed for $40 a week, including breakfast and dinner — and Hazel Sinclair was famous far beyond Kittery for her fine cooking. The Portsmouth Black Heritage Trail has recently assumed a lease on the property, which still remains in the Sinclair family.

The final spot on your tour lies another mile further north on the LEFT, at 199 Brave Boat Harbor Road. (36) The **Philbrook Farm** sits up on a hill overlooking the harbor and salt-marshes. The cape house is about 200 years old with a great old barn. Fernalds built the complex and Philbrooks farmed here for nearly one hundred years.

If you look out to the harbor and to the RIGHT you will see a small outbuilding that was the cabin of the handyman at the farm from 1927 to 1942. There is a small parking spot on the RIGHT, where a **National Wildlife Refuge** sign is posted.

You are now at the York town line and this driving tour of Kittery and Kittery Point has come to an end. The area is so scenic that wandering on your own is recommended. Do be particularly careful, however, whenever you stop. In summer, bicycles proliferate.

Photographer Neil Troost's comments on taking this truly breath-taking image: In mid-March of 1999, a stiff northeast gale was creating some big waves, many of which were breaking dramatically against Whaleback Light, off Kittery Point, Maine. Obstacles such as salt spray, snowdrifts, a very cold and raw wind, and very thick clouds made getting this image difficult. Racing against the receding tide, I shot a few frames on each promising wave series. The trick was catching the sunlight, breaking through the thick clouds, and illuminating the lighthouse while a good wave was breaking. I was well rewarded with this image!

EIGHT "MUST SEE" PLACES THAT EVERYONE IN KITTERY AND KITTERY POINT HAS BEEN TO

This chapter in our Guide Book features eight businesses that are each unique and yet are the essence of Kittery. They share lots of similarities. All but one has something to do with food. All except Frisbee's, which opened in 1828, were started just before or after the Second World War, and all have expanded, expanded and expanded again. From humble origins, they have become the thriving enterprises you find today.

BOB'S CLAM HUT
US Route 1, Kittery, ME 03904
207-439-4233; www.bobsclamhut.com

Bob's Clam Hut, great casual dining in the midst of the Kittery Outlet Malls.

The Bob's Clam Hut of today differs greatly from the modest seasonal business begun in 1956. Back then Bob Kraft was given a piece of his parents' back yard on Route 1 to open a clam shack. Until then he had driven a taxi and worked in the kitchen of a Portsmouth restaurant, where in a bold move, he tossed out the standard recipe for preparing clams and substituted his own. (He was a great fan of El's Clams further up the road in York). The boss called him in and, instead of the expected criticism, he was greeted with these words: "Best clams I've ever eaten!!" And that's what people are still saying.

There have been many changes since those early days of takeout seasonal service. Bob and his wife, Betty, and their children ran the business for thirty years. It was like a town meeting on Friday nights for local Kittery people who would line up outside in cars or at the picnic tables and discuss politics and the weather. Legend has it that Betty would see who was coming and prepare their food even before their order was placed. Bob's Clam Hut has never experienced a bad year and remains as popular as ever.

Michael Landgarten, musician, song writer and computer person, purchased the restaurant in 1986, responding to a family friend's suggestion he come to Kittery and check out Bob's Clam Hut which was for sale. His way of checking it out was to work there for a day. That's all it took! He loved it and has been deeply involved with it ever since.

The Krafts continued their interest in the Clam Hut and provided training and guidance to the new owner for the first couple of years. Now the business has grown and expanded to six times the volume of 1986. Michael has worked to maintain the concern's original spirit and values, its great quality seafood, family environment, and loyalty between staff and ownership. Bob's Clam Hut has won lots of praise in national food magazines and newspapers for having the "best clams around."

 CHAUNCEY CREEK LOBSTER PIER
Chauncey Creek Road, Kittery Point. ME 03905
207-439-1030; www.chaunceycreek.com

The ever popular Chauncey Creek Lobster Pier started out with lobsterman Herb Witham selling lobsters from his pier on Chauncey Creek to friends and neighbors before delivering his main catch to commercial dealers and markets. Herb's nephew, George Spinney, fished as a teenager with his uncle and, in time, was able to buy his own boat. World War II intervened (George spent the war years in the Coast Guard), but by 1945 he was back lobstering.

Chauncey Creek, a summer favorite of locals and tourists in the know.

In the meantime, Herb had added a soft drink cooler and lobster rolls to the menu, satifying customers' requests for cooked lobsters as well. George's new wife, Claire, became chief lobster roll maker, managing the pier while Herb and George fished. In those days, lobster rolls cost 65 cents; a cup of coffee went for a dime. When Claire and George made changes to modernize things, Uncle Herb would grumble, but soon would be heard to say, "Yup, the Boy and I did that!"

By the 1950s the pier was a popular hargout for local young people who swam, water-skied and entertained the customers by jumping off the roof. Several generations of local youngsters got their first taste of work with summer jobs at the Chauncey Creek. At the end of the working day, with the right tide, everyone went in swimming, Claire included. On a dare, she once jumped in, "white pants and all!" (She told lingering customers that was how she laundered them.) Claire was even known to go in after a little boy who'd fallen in.

Herb Witham died in 1969, and Claire and George Spinney took over the business, running it until 1984. They, in turn, sold it to their son, Ron, and his wife, Jean. The older Spinneys continue to be invaluable helpers. More changes came over the years, including additions to the once very simple menu. Along with lobsters and lobster rolls, Chauncey Creek now offers a raw bar, chicken, hot dogs, beans, corn, crab rolls and much more. The real charm of sitting at tables at the water's edge, eating perfectly-cooked lobsters in the fresh air while watching the sun go down, will forever remain the same: QUINTESSENTIALLY MAINE!

⭐ CARL'S MEAT MARKET
25 U S Route 1, Kittery, ME 03904
207-439-1557

Carl's Meat Market is one of the favorite stops on what has become known as Kittery's Gourmet Alley.

The crew at today's Carl's Meat Market.

Early in the 20th century, Carl Peschel emigrated from Germany, taking a job in the meat business in Portsmouth before striking out on his own. He started his market in the late 1930s, in the front part of his modest house on nearby Government Street, and included delicatessen offerings. Navy Yard workers would stop for lunch sandwiches. Carl's, it was said, had a little bit of everything.

Carl died in 1949 and there was a lull in the life of the meat market until his son, Ken, returned from the Armed Service. One story says he came home with three hundred dollars in his pocket and headed straight into Portsmouth to buy meat with that money. He and his wife, Hilda, reopened the business in the same location on Government Street, where they continued to operate until 1979 when Frank Belleville became the new owner. In 1982, Frank moved the business to US Route 1 beside the Golden Harvest, where it can be found today, providing quality meats and poultry, and once again, treats from the deli for the people of Kittery and well beyond. Carl's Meat Market lives up to its 75-year repution for having "a little bit of everything!"

 FRISBEE'S MARKET & CAP'N SIMEON'S GALLEY
90 Pepperrell Road (Route 103), Kittery Point, ME 03905
207-439-3655; www.capnsimeons.com

Sixth-generation family members can be found behind the counter at today's Frisbee's Market.

The Frisbee family has operated Frisbee's Store since 1828. The oldest grocery store in the United States run by succeeding generations of the same family, and the only store in Kittery Point in the 19th century, Frisbee's naturally became the gathering point for locals and visitors. In the old store, everyone gathered around the pot-bellied stove to talk and play checkers.

The current Frisbees' great-great-great grandfather, Daniel, and their uncle, still referred to as "Mr. Williams," were the original owners. The property had been purchased from the Cutts family which had obtained it from the U.S. government after the American Revolution. It was confiscated from Sir William Pepperrell II (his house still stands next door) who, as a leading Loyalist, moved to England to retain his title. The building itself had been built in 1680 and had housed a marine store.

One of the Frisbee great-grandmothers all those years ago was Joanna Pepperrell Jackson, sister of Sir William Pepperrell. Joanna's daughter married into the Gerrish Family and the rest, as they say, is history. The present generation's grandfather, Solon, was always quoted as saying, "Yes we have it. Now what is it you want?"

In 1915, a new structure was built next to the original store but closer to the highway (now Route 103), which winds its way through Kittery Point. Soon after, gasoline pumps were installed to service those new-fangled "horseless carriages." In 1953, the Frisbee family renovated the store. The wharf, once owned by the family, was given to the town in 1954; the Frisbee heirs still retain business rights on the wharf today.

Frisbee's isn't shy about touting its status as oldest family-run business in the United States.

Deciding to open a restaurant in 1969, the Frisbees cast about for a name and remembered George S. Wasson's novel, written in 1903, *Cap'n Simeon's Store*. It was based on the actual Frisbee's Store. The opening page reads:

> Every evening with sublime indifference to the weather, numerous citizens of the Cove may be seen plodding down the winding road leading to Cap'n Simeon's...

This was the name they chose for the new restaurant directly behind the store. This 19th century classic tale of a small New England community reflects the importance of hospitality. Their goal was to maintain that same generosity of spirit and great food as the fictional Cap'n Simeon's.

GOLDEN HARVEST PRODUCE MARKET
US Route 1, Kittery, ME 03904
207-439-2113

The Golden Harvest, where neighbor catches up with neighbor over the muskmelons and beans.

Golden Harvest Produce Market has a rich history of providing the best vegetables and fruits in the area. Nick Pelluso, the original owner, sold produce from the back of his truck in Atlantic Heights, one of Portsmouth's neighborhoods, in the 1950s, before leasing the land on US Route 1 in Kittery where the market remains today. In 1960, he opened his seasonal store with just two stalls, specializing in produce from local farmers. He gradually expanded, bought the land in the early 1970s, and the business became year-round. Buying cheese and dry goods from outside vendors, he continued to get his produce locally whenever possible. His customers waited for fresh corn ("Picked Today!"), peaches, apples, tomatoes, etc., as the seasons warranted. He also provided fresh produce for local restaurants seven days a week and became the largest distributor on the Seacoast.

In 1998, Jim and Carla Spencer purchased the Golden Harvest with the agreement that Nick would stay on and teach them the business for a year. This happy arrangement lasted more like two years, with Nick coming and going freely and mentoring the new owners. The market has thrived under their direction, keeping many of the original staff. Jim and Carla have made some changes, adding wines, specialty cheeses and an appetizing salad bar for take-out, and doing all the dry goods in house. They continue to offer as much local produce as possible, making a daily truck run into Boston as well. One of the first stores on what is now known as Gourmet Alley, the Golden Harvest is the most important stop for most of Kittery's fine food shoppers.

 KITTERY TRADING POST
US Route 1, Kittery, ME 03904
207-439-2700
www.kitterytradingpost.com

Philip (Bing) Adams acquired the Kittery Trading Post in 1938, at the time a modest one-room trading post/gas station. In the early days, Bing's reputation as an "honest horse trader" brought people from far and wide to swap fur pelts for gas and beef for ammunition and supplies for a car.

In 1961, Bing's son, Kevin, bought the store, allowing Bing to enjoy the Maine woods as he had taught others to do for nearly 25 years. The gas pumps are gone now but the floor space had been gradually expanded to the 42,000 square feet we know today.

Despite the fact that Kevin was only 21 years old when he took over, he did not lack experience in the family business, having worked in the store for his father off and on since the age of ten. The years of 1961 through 1971 were filled with continuous renovation and expansion. One thing never changed, however: quality of service and great prices offered to customers.

In 1986, after dedicating many years to expanding the family business and increasing sales, Kevin, like his father, decided it was time to retire. He, too, wanted to enjoy the out-of-doors as he had been helping others to do for over 25 years. A new family consortium was formed to purchase the business, determined to carry on the family's commitment of offering quality service to people who loved the great outdoors.

In 2003, as a result of customer demand and company growth, the retail space was expanded yet again. Construction began in January and the grand opening took place in September 2005. Today, with a staff of over 300 employees, Kittery Trading Post sells everything from ski jackets to balsam pine pillows. Although no longer a one-room gas station, the family values of quality service, competitive prices and exceptional selection remain intact. What started as one man's dream has turned into what is now known as the Kittery Trading Post Tradition!

You'll find everything for the great outdoors on three levels of the most extensive selection of outdoor recreational equipment, clothing and footwear in New England.

From humble beginnings to 42,000 square feet of retail space, the story of the Kittery Trading Post is chapter one of the story of the Kittery Outlet Malls, the oldest outlet area in the United States.

⭐ WARREN'S LOBSTER HOUSE
11 Water Street, Kittery, ME 03904
207-439-1630; www.lobsterhouse.com

Franklin Roosevelt was in the White House and the winds of war were blowing across Europe in 1940 when Warren "Pete" Wurm added a walk-up window and six stools to his existing wholesale lobster business on the Kittery wharf. In those days, you could buy lobster for 25 cents a pound.

The Warren's sign has been welcoming folks to Maine for generations.

For the next 15 years, Pete operated a business that gradually expanded and added to the building. Those six stools grew to a 150 seat restaurant. The story goes that Pete's brother was the warden at the then still-active Portsmouth Naval Prison. When fill was needed to expand the restaurant area, which was under water at the time where the parking lot is now, both labor and material, in the form of rocks, were made available.

In 1955, Warren's was sold to Edmund Anton, the owner of Anton's in Manchester, and Fred Assad. The two men and their families operated the restaurant until 1984. During the 19 years of their ownership they added a 32 seat bar, and in 1978 the popular salad bar was installed with 40 selections. This salad bar proved to be one

BUSINESSES

of the most distinctive and well-remembered features of Warren's. Business partners Scott Cunningham and Dave Mickee bought Warren's in 1984. Graduates of Penn State in Hotel and Restaurant Management, Scott and Dave met when they worked in the food services business and found they shared a common goal. Each had always wanted to own a restaurant. Both men felt it was very important to maintain the essential quality in Warren's because it had already become a destination.

Scott and Dave's first decision was to make Warren's a year-round restaurant, breaking the seasonal cycle and enabling them to keep staff all year. They installed air-conditioning and added items to the salad bar, now maxed out with 60 choices. In 1988, they added the 56-seat solarium and then, in 1994, the enclosed deck where 60 guests can now enjoy 'almost' outdoor seating despite the well-known whims of New England weather.

 WEATHERVANE SEAFOOD RESTAURANT & MARKET
306 US Route 1, Kittery, ME 03904
207-439-0316; www.weathervaneseafoods.com

Across the street from the Kittery Trading Post is a thriving seafood restaurant, the original of sixteen Weathervanes owned by Terry Gagner and his family, with locations as far south as Plymouth, MA, as far west as Saratoga, NY, and as far north as Belfast, ME.

Weathervane's corporate headquarters are located in an impressive building on Badger's Island overlooking the Piscataqua River. The company now employs 150 locally and 1750 overall, selling half a million pounds of lobsters a year and shipping everywhere in the world. Many of those lobsters come across their dock on Badger's Island from local fishermen.

Terry Gagner's parents, Ray and Bea, were living on Cape Cod when Bea decided to open a clam shack. In 1959 the couple left the Cape and returned to Kittery where Bea's father, James B. Trefethen, lived. There she again opened another clam shack, this time on the site of what had been a Chinese restaurant, across from the Kittery Trading Post on Route 1.

The Gagner's original business was seasonal and only offered

The Weathervane, another fine business that got its start in Kittery.

take-out service. Bea and Ray continued to run the business until 1976 when Terry and his wife, Janet, took over the reins. It became a full service restaurant in the 1970s.

In 1978, Weathervane began expanding, opening a second restaurant in Dover, NH, followed in 1979 by a third in Sanford, ME. Over the years, Weathervane has become the major Seacoast business one finds today. All this from a little seasonal takeout clam shack begun in the 1960s — and after years of hard work.

5 NEW BUSINESSES
ON KITTERY'S "GOURMET ALLEY"

A nd here are the "must visit" NEW places that everyone in Kittery and Kittery Point is buzzing about now and will be talking about for years to come.

 ### BEACH PEA BAKING COMPANY
53 State Road, U S Route 1, Kittery, ME 03904
207-439-3555

Super gourmet breads of all kinds, plus the most delicious pastries. Stop by for soup, sandwiches and salad - and do treat yourself to a dessert you won't soon forget.

 ### TERRA COTTA PASTA
52 State Road, U S Route 1, Kittery, ME 03904
207-475-3025

Not just fresh, homemade pasta and ravioli, but sauces, salads, calzone-style "tarts," creative soups and delicious breads as well.

 ### CACAO CHOCOLATE
64 Government Street, Kittery, ME 03904
207-438-9001

A chocolatier extraordinaire, with handmade truffles and other utterly decadent treats. Would you believe a gorganzola-and-curried-walnut truffle?

 ### ENOTECA ITALIANA
122 U S Route 1, Kittery, ME 03904
207-439-7216

An exceptional selection of the finest cheeses, meats, delicacies and wines, beers and liquers, all imported directly from Italy.

 ### PAPERS, INK!
64 Wallingford Square, Kittery, ME 03904
207-439-1955

Featuring a no-holds-barred collection of great paper goods, gifts and select books, all with an attitude.

LISTS

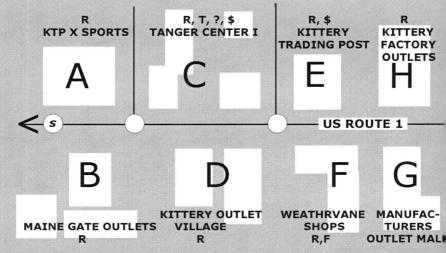

THE KITTERY MALLS

| R
KTP X SPORTS
A | R, T, ?, $
TANGER CENTER I
C | R, $
**KITTERY
TRADING POST**
E | R
**KITTERY
FACTORY
OUTLETS**
H |

←S————○——————————○————— **US ROUTE 1**

B | **D** | **F** | **G**

MAINE GATE OUTLETS | **KITTERY OUTLET** | **WEATHRVANE** | **MANUFAC-**
R | **VILLAGE** | **SHOPS** | **TURERS**
| **R** | **R,F** | **OUTLET MALL**

R - RESTROOMS   ? - INFORMATION

CLOTHING

J	Aeropostale	451-9400
D	Anne Klein	439-5238
I	Appleseed's	439-7775
O	Banana Republic	451-9011
N	Big Dog Sportswear	439-4101
M	Brooks Brothers	439-5533
D	Calvin Klein	438-9598
N	Casual Male Big & Tall	439-8510
C	Coldwater Creek Outlet	439-5456
C	Dana Buchman/Ellen Tracy	439-3073
J	Dress Barn	439-6293
J	Dress Barn Woman	439-7873
B	Eddie Bauer	439-7749
O	Gap Outlet	439-5712
I	Geoffrey Beene	439-4427
O	Hickey Freeman	439-8350
J	Izod	439-7040
D	J. Crew	439-5810
G	Jones New York	439-5873
C	Jones New York Country	439-4747
D	Jones N Y Suits	439-1442
J	Kasper	439-1067
A	Kittery Trading Post	888-587-6246
C	Liz Claiborne Outlet	439-9955
C	Liz Claiborne Women	439-0551
H	Maidenform	439-2270
J	Motherhood Maternity	439-1729
M	Nautica	439-1551
O	Old Navy	439-1963
O	PacSun	439-4944
D	Polo Ralph Lauren	439-6664
J	Puma	438-9660

K	Rue 21	438-9229
J	Timberland	439-6323
J	Tommy Hilfiger	439-8880
C	Van Heusen	439-6020
K	Van Heusen	439-0045
J	Wilsons Leather	438-9459

CHILDREN'S

C	Carter's Childrenswear	439-4618
O	Hanna Andersson	439-1992
I	Hartstrings Childrenswear	439-0600
J	KB Toys	439-3542
C	OshKosh	439-9279
J	The Children's Outlet	439-0185

FOOTWEAR

C	Bass Clothing & Shoe	439-4277
O	Clarks Bostonian	439-4300
J	Cole Haan	439-0555
J	Easy Spirit	439-0151
G	Ecco	438-9551
H	Etienne Aigner	439-6886
H	Factory Brand Shoes	439-3484
J	Naturalizer	439-4208
B	Nine West	439-9417
O	Reebok	439-5100
O	Rockport	439-0090
G	Saucony	439-8071
M	Skechers	439-0556
K	Stride-Rite/Keds/ SperryTopsider	439-8444
L	Super Shoes	439-3667

THE KITTERY MALLS

R, T, ?, $, F
MAINE OUTLETS

R, T
OUTLET MALL OF KITTERY

R, $
TIDEWATER MALL

J   N   L   O

N →

I   K   M   P

KITTERY PLACE

KITTERY OUTLET CENTER

TANGER CENTER II
R

TANGER CENTER III

R, T, $, F

F - FOOD   T - TELEPHONE $ - ATM

ACCESSORIES & LUGGAGE

O	Coach	439-5915
J	Jockey	439-8221
J	L'eggs Hanes Bali Playtex	439-7052
C	L'eggs Hanes Bali Playtex	439-5433
M	Samsonite	439-3500
J	Samsonite	439-4700
N	Sox Market, Inc.	439-1967
J	Sunglass Hut	439-5942
K	Totes/Sunglass World	439-4511
H	Tumi	439-6531

FOOD

I	Burger King	439-5516
J	McDonald's of Kittery	439-0301
J	Noel's Café & Coffee Shop	439-0711
F	Pepperidge Farm	439-6051
G	Starbucks	451-9701
F	Weathervane Seafood Rest.	439-0330
F	" Fish Market & Take Out	439-0316

HOUSEWARES/HOME

N	Cape Cod Crafters	439-8780
B	Corningware Corelle Revere	439-6363
K	Crate and Barrel	439-8600
K	Cuddledown	439-8800
O	Foreside Company	439-4600
J	Fuller Brush	439-0206
M	Kitchen Collection	439-7556
C	Le Creuset	439-4811
J	Le Gourmet Chef	451-2157
O	Lenox	439-0232

J	Linens 'N Things	439-4125
J	Mikasa	439-6550
J	Oneida Home	439-1949
O	Pfaltzgraff	439-4728
O	Reed & Barton	439-4907
K	Royal Doulton Outlet	439-4760
M	Villeroy & Boch	439-6440
J	Waterford Wedgwood	439-6558
J	Welcome Home	438-9295

OTHER SPECIALTIES

C	Black & Decker	439-5681
I	Book Warehouse	439-8551
G	Bose	439-5577
J	Brookstone	439-2937
I	Claire Murray	438-9371
J	Cosmetic Company	438-9275
J	Greater York Chamber of Commerce Welcome Center	439-2576
K	Harry and David	438-9675
A	KTP X Sports	888-587-6246
H	Lindt Factory Store	451-9772
J	Movado Company Store	439-8772
P	Nextel	438-9350
J	Perfumania	439-9891
K	Ross-Simons Jewelers	451-9800
I	Russell Stover Candies	439-2900
K	Seiko	439-5481
N	The Sweatshirt Shop	439-9731
G	Yankee Candle	439-5700
O	Zales Fine Jewelry	439-0205

Kittery Trading Post   888-587-6246

KITTERY LODGING

BED & BREAKFASTS

Chickadee Bed and Breakfast
    63 Haley Road, Kittery, ME 03904
    207-439-0672 or toll free: 888-502-0876
    www.bbonline.com/me/chickadee
    e-mail access from the web site
Enchanted Nights Bed and Breakfast
    29 Wentworth Street, Kittery, ME 03904
    207-439-1489
    www.enchantednights.com
Portsmouth Harbor Inn and Spa
    6 Water Street, Kittery, ME 03904
    207-439-4040
    www.innatportsmouth.com
    e-mail: info@innatportsmouth.com

MOTELS & INNS

Blue Roof Motel
    US Route 1 By-Pass, Kittery, ME 03904
    207-439-9324
Coachman Inn
    380 US Route 1, Kittery, ME 03904
    207-439-4434 or toll free: 800-824-6183
    www.coachmaninn.net
    e-mail access from the web site
Litson Villas
    127 US Route 1, Kittery, ME 03904
    207-439-5000 or toll free: 800-966-8455
    www.litson-villas.com
    e-mail: smiles@litson-villas.com
Northeaster Motel
    79 Old Post Road, Kittery, ME 03904
    207-439-0116
    www.northeastermotel.com

Rex Motel
>US Route 1 By-Pass, Kittery, ME 03904
>207-439-9002

Rodeway Inn
>US Route 1 By-Pass, Kittery, ME 03904
>207-439-5555
>www.choicemotels.com
>e-mail: gm.me053.com

Super 8 Motel
>U S Route 1 By-Pass, Kittery, ME 03904
>207-439-2000
>www.super8.com
>e-mail: access from the web site.

View from the Town Dock at Cap'n Simeon's.

KITTERY FOOD IN ALL FORMS

Anneke Jans
60 Wallingford Square, Kittery, ME 03904
207-439-0001; www.annekejans.net

Bagel Caboose
Kittery Traffic Circle, 176 US Route 1, Kittery, ME 03904
207-439-5099

Bob's Clam Hut
US Route 1, Kittery, ME 03904
207-439-4233; www.bobsclamhut.com

Burger King Restaurant
US Route 1, Kittery, ME 03904
207-439-5516

Cap'n Simeon's Galley
Pepperrell Road, Kittery Point, ME 03905
207-439-3655; www.capnsimeons.com

Chauncey Creek Lobster Pier
Chauncey Creek Road, Kittery Point, ME 03905
207-439-1030; www.chaunceycreek.com

Chun Ping Lau
436 US Route 1, Kittery, ME 03904
207-439-6055

Crooked Lane Café
70 Wallingford Square, Kittery, ME 03904
207-439-2244

Dairy Queen
Kittery Traffic Circle, 174 US Route 1, Kittery, Me 03904
207-439-4949; seasonal

Divine Cuisines
2 Government Street, Kittery, ME 03904
207-451-9511

The Dog House
181 US Route 1, Kittery, ME 03904
207-439-1559

Loco Coco's Tacos
36 Walker Street, Kittery, ME 03904
207-438-9322

McDonalds Restaurant
US Route 1, Kittery, ME 03904
207-439-0301

Navy Yard Bar & Billiards
182 US Route 1, Kittery, ME 03904
207-439-7135

Noels Restaurant & Bakery
US Route 1, Maine Outlet Mall, Kittery, ME 03904
207-439-0711

Payrin Restaurant
182 US Route 1, Kittery, ME 03904
207-439-6536

Robert's Maine Grill & Market
326 US Route 1, Kittery, ME 03904
207-439-0300; www.robertsmainegrill.com

Subway Sandwich & Salad
US Route 1, Kittery, ME 03904
207-439-8511

Sunrise Grill
182 US Route 1, Kittery, ME 03904
207-439-5748

Town Pizza Restaurant
15 Wentworth Street, Kittery, ME 03904
207-439-1265

Warren's Lobster House
11 Water Street, Kittery, ME 03904; 207-439-1630
www.lobsterhouse.com

Weathervane Lobster in the Rough
31 Badger's Island West, Kittery, ME 03904
207-439-0335, Ext. 126; Seasonal May-October
www.weathervaneseafoods.com

Weathervane Seafood Restaurant
306 US Route 1, Kittery, ME 03904
207-439-0330; www.weathervaneseafoods.com

York's Best Seafood
US Route 1, Kittery, ME 03904
207-439-3401

PLACES OF WORSHIP

KITTERY

Church of Christ
48 Love Lane, Kittery, ME 03904
207-439-0720
Founded 1958

First Baptist Church
22 Litchfield Road, Kittery, ME 03904
207-439-1200; www.fbckittery.org
Founded 1975

St. Mark's United Methodist Church
60 Government Street, Kittery, ME 03904
207-439-9686
Founded 1864

St. Raphael's Parish
6 Whipple Road, Kittery, ME 03904
207-439-0442; e-mail: Saintraphaels@comcast.net.
Founded 1916

Second Christian Congregational Church UCC
33 Government Street, Kittery, ME 03904
207-439-3903; www.secondchristianchurch.com
Founded 1843

The Church at Spruce Creek
31 Wilson Road, Kittery, ME 03904
207-439-4598; www.sprucecreekchurch.org.
Founded 1802

Jehovah's Witnesses Kingdom Hall
14 Dennett Road, Kittery, ME 03904
207-439-0007

KITTERY POINT

First Baptist Church of Kittery Point
636 Haley Road, Kittery Point, ME 03905
207-439-4077

First Christian Church
542 Haley Road, Kittery Point, ME 03905
207-439-4021
Founded 1806

First Congregational Church of Kittery at Kittery Point, UCC

First Congregational Church of Kittery at Kittery Point, UCC
23 Pepperrell Road, Kittery Point, ME 03905
207-439-0650; www.kitterypointucc.org
Founded 1714

KITTERY SCHOOLS

Schooling in Kittery began informally in the 18th century. As the area developed, so did the schools, beginning in homes, then moving into one-room schoolhouses that evolved into more complex institutions. Today, the community has 2 elementary-level buildings, a middle school and a high school. The Kittery School Department is located in the Town Hall at 200 Rogers Road (207-439-6819). The website address for the Kittery school system is www.kitteryschools.org.

The **Mitchell Primary School** teaches youngsters in Kindergarten through 2nd grade. It is located on School Lane off Haley Road up behind the fire station in Kittery Point. The school was named for community figure, politician and Superintendent of Schools, Horace Mitchell (see page **6**). There is an active Parent-Teacher Association at Mitchell School. The phone number is 207-439-1707.

Frisbee Elementary School, at 120 Rogers Road, is for students in grades 3 through 5. The phone number is 207-439-1122. Frank C. Frisbee was a prominent Kittery citizen. Frisbee School shares an active PTA with Mitchell School.

The **Shapleigh Middle School** serves students in grades 6 through 8. The Shapleigh complex is located on the crossroads of Stevenson and Manson Roads in northern Kittery. The phone number is 207-439-2572. The school is named for Harriet Shapleigh, a veteran teacher, and Dr. Edward Shapleigh, a respected citizen. The middle school has a PTA.

The **Robert W. Traip Academy** is a public high school that serves grades 9 through 12. Enrollment in the 2005-2006 school year is 350 students. Traip is accredited by the New England Association of Schools & Colleges. In addition to their regular studies, all students must complete the "Preparation for Citizenship" civics class. Twenty hours of community service are also required for graduation.

The school's benefactor, Robert W. Traip, was a successful businessman born in Kittery in the section of town called Kittery

Foreside. In 1864, when he died, his will left money to procure suitable buildings for the purpose of establishing an academy in Kittery (see page 65). Traip Academy opened in 1905 and graduated its first class of two students in 1906. Traip Academy is located at 12 Williams Avenue in Kittery Foreside. The phone is 207-439-1121.

The **Kittery Adult Education Program** offers opportunities for completing a high school diploma or GED certificate, as well as a variety of enrichment classes in the evenings. The office is located at the Traip Academy, 12 Williams Avenue. The phone number is 207-439-5896.

The local **Head Start**, a federally funded pre-school program, is based in the Frisbee building. The program is tuition-free for income-eligible children. The phone number is 207-438-9306.

As of this publication, there are no private schools within Kittery. Pre-schools and daycare facilities are listed in the yellow pages.

If you take the driving tour (pages 62-76), you will see some older school buildings of interest. The Wentworth-Dennett grade school, a 3-story brick building on the north corner of US Route 1 and Government Street, now houses artists' studios. (See Map 1 on page 58, #3; photo page 64.) Often you can see large sculptures on the lawn. The Austin School, built in 1875 on Whipple Road (Route 103), is painted a bright red; you cannot miss it. The school is a private home now. (See Map 2, page 59, #15; photos pages 7 and 67.) Further along Route 103 on the Brave Boat Harbor Road section, the Stafford School stands on the corner of Cutts Island Lane. (See Map 4, page 61, #34; photo page 75.) Built as a one-room schoolhouse, the two-door entrance is still obvious in this private dwelling.

KITTERY TOWN GOVERNMENT

When Maine entered the Union in 1820, there were only 240 incorporated towns in the state. Today the state consists of nearly 500 municipalities.

There are two basic forms of government in Maine: the "direct" form, referred to as the town meeting form of government, in which the town meeting serves as the legislative body, passing laws and approving the spending of money; and the "representational" form, in which an elected council serves as the legislative body.

There are five basic variations within these two forms of government:

> Town Meeting/Selectmen
> Town Meeting/Selectmen and Manager
> Council-Town Meeting/Manager
> Council/Manager
> Council/Mayor and Administrator

Kittery has a Council/Manager form of government. The council, an elected body, serves both the legislative and executive functions. Unlike the town meeting form, the Council/Manager form must be adopted through the local charter. Kittery has six town councilors, a town attorney and a town manager.

In 2006, Kittery's town manager is **Jonathan Carter**. Town Hall is located just off the Kittery Traffic Circle at 200 Rogers Road. The phone number is 207-439-0452.

IMPORTANT PHONE NUMBERS

EMERGENCY Fire, Police, Ambulance 9-1-1
Poison Control Center 1-800-222-1222

Other Police Business
        200 Rogers Road, Kittery . . . . (207) 439-1638
Town Hall
        200 Rogers Road, Kittery . . . . (207) 439-0452
Harbor Master
        76 Pocahontas Road, Kittery . . . . . (207) 439-0912
Highway Auto Repair & Towing
        US Route 1, Kittery . . . .(207) 439-4100
Kittery Animal Hospital
        195 State Road, Kittery . . . . (207) 439-4158
Piscataqua Animal Hospital
        103 US Route 1, Kittery . . . . (207) 439-9707
Rice Public Library
        8 Wentworth Street, Kittery . . . . . (207) 439-1553
Kittery Recreation Department
        2 Cole Street, Kittery. . . . . (207) 439-3800
Frisbee School
        120 Rogers Road . . . .(207) 439-1122
Horace Mitchell School
        Pepperrell Road, Kittery . . . . (207) 439-1707
Shapleigh School
        Manson Road, Kittery . . . .(207) 439-2572
Traip Academy
        Williams Avenue, Kittery . . . .(207) 439-1121

*From Kittery, calls to the following towns are charged at
local rates:
        Area Code 207: Eliot, South Berwick, York
        Area Code 603: Portsmouth, New Castle, Newington,
                        Greenland, Rye and Rye Beach
*ZIP codes: Kittery, 03904; Kittery Point, 03905

FOOD FOR
AN AUGUST DINNER

If you come from Kittery, you probably can skip this next chapter. You've made this dinner many times, especially when visitors arrive from the Midwest. This is an August dinner, complete with fresh boiled lobsters, fresh corn on the cob, a nice green salad and for dessert, a homemade blueberry pie. For those not from Kittery, here is how it is done.

BUYING LOBSTERS
We thought we should sketch out what to do with those really good, fresh lobsters when you get them home. Buy them the day of your dinner. (See page 107 at the end of this section on where to shop for lobster.)

Size	Pounds	Cooking Time
Chicken	1 pound	10 minutes
Quarters	under 1½ lb.	10 minutes
Large	1 ½ to 2 ½ lbs.	15 minutes
Jumbo	over 2 ½ lbs.	20 minutes

Lobsters come either "hard shell" or "soft shell." Hard shell are the more traditional, while soft shell are slightly less expensive and, some think, easier to open. There is no difference in taste. Smaller lobsters are more tender because you cook them for less time. A raw green lobster turns red as it cooks.

THINGS TO KNOW BEFORE YOU START
A lobster dinner at home can be a bit messy. Use a cotton table cloth that can be easily washed or a paper table cloth to throw away after dinner. The chief cook should have an apron on and plenty of paper towels at the ready. Place large empty bowls on the table for the discarded lobster shells.

1. In the largest pot you own, bring water to a boil. Some say that sea water is best. However, sea water is difficult to come by unless you are right on the beach, and it takes much longer to boil. Besides, the lobsters don't really care and if you want salt water, you can always just add salt to your pot of fresh water.

1a. You can also steam lobsters with 2 inches of water in the bottom of the pot. The cooking times are the same. Be sure not to let the water boil out of the pot.

2. Plunge live lobsters head first into the boiling water and, no, they do not cry. Cook according to the size of the lobsters (see chart above). Do NOT over-cook.

3. Remove the cooked lobsters, now bright red, from the pot. Use tongs — they will be *very* hot.

4. This is the messy part. Lay the lobster on its back on a cutting board. With a sharp knife, stab it in the chest and cut down toward the tail. With both hands (wear cooking mitts - it's still hot), open the body cavity and expose the tail meat. With a small knife, remove its dark line of intestine. Then drain it over the sink. Lots of liquid will come out. Put the lobster on a plate and serve it to your guests. Save the green liver or "tomalley" and the pink roe or "coral." These are great delicacies.

If you don't have lobster "crackers" or "pickers" (available at any cooking supply store), a small hammer will do nicely. Kitchen shears work well, too. One cannot get at the meat in the legs and claws without smashing them open and picking the meat out.

Even the small legs, four to a side, have tasty bites inside. Twist a leg off the body. Put the whole leg ¾ of the way in your mouth, open end first, and bite down firmly with your front teeth. Then, while pulling the leg out of your mouth, maneuver the meat to the end of its shell where it finally arrives on your tongue. Children are particularly adept at this.

Lobster is best served with a small pot of melted butter. Some like a squirt of lemon juice in their butter. Others take their butter neat, or just prefer a straight squeeze of lemon.

CORN ON THE COB

Shucking corn is best done outside. This is another skill at which children excel.

Drop the corn into your second largest pot of boiling salted water. Cover the pot and return it to boiling. Then turn off the heat and wait 5 minutes.

Remove the corn from the water with tongs and place on a platter. Drape with a kitchen towel to keep warm. Serve with butter and salt. Two ears per person are customary, but when the corn is as fresh as fresh local corn can be, all bets are off.

BLUEBERRY PIE

For those who know how and enjoy making fresh pastry dough, roll out enough for a two-crust pie. For the rest of us, refrigerated, ready-to-use pie crusts make a perfectly acceptable substitute. Follow directions on the package. You will need two crusts.

For blueberries, the very small, wild blueberries of August are the best. Frozen blueberries will do just fine for the rest of the year.

Ingredients:
- 3 tablespoons of flour
- 1 cup of sugar
- 1/8 teaspoon of salt
- 4 cups or so of blueberries
- 1 tablespoon of lemon juice
- 1 tablespoon of butter

Preheat your oven to 425° F, with the rack positioned in the middle. Line the the bottom of your pie plate with half of the pastry dough and trim. Mix the flour, sugar and salt in a large bowl. Add the washed (if fresh) or defrosted blueberries and lemon juice to the mixture and toss together. Pile the berry mixture into the pie plate and dot with butter. Put the second crust on top. Crimp, flute or pinch together around the edge of the pie plate and don't forget to cut several vents or small holes in the top.

Bake for 10 minutes, then lower the oven to 350° F and continue cooking 30 to 40 minutes longer. Your pie can be baked in the morning or even the day before. Put it in the ice-box (that's a refrigerator, for you younger folk) if you do your baking the day before.

OPTIONAL TOPPINGS

Many think that a classic blueberry pie is delicious on its own. However, others prefer it topped with whipped cream or a scoop of vanilla ice cream.

WHERE TO PURCHASE YOUR LIVE MAINE LOBSTERS

Morrison's Lobster, 11 Badger's Island West, Kittery, ME 03904
439-2501; seasonal, gift shop

Robert's Maine Grill & Market, 326 US Route 1, Kittery, ME 03904
207-439-0300; www.robertsmainegrill..com

Seaview Lobster Co., 43 Government Street, Kittery, ME 03904
439-1599; www.seaviewlobster.com
Only live lobsters, will ship

Sue's Seafood, 33 Old Post Road (Route 103), Kittery, ME
439-5608

Taylor Lobster Co., 32 Route 236, Kittery, ME
439-1350; www.taylorlobster.com
Also fresh fish, will ship

Warren's Lobster House, Water Street, Kittery, ME
439-1630; www.lobsterhouse.com
All year round, will ship, gift shop

INDEX

NOTES

NOTES

NOTES